EASY ASIAN COOKBOOK

200 ASIAN RECIPES FROM THAILAND, KOREA, JAPAN, INDONESIA, VIETNAM, AND THE PHILIPPINES

By
Chef Maggie Chow
Copyright © 2015 by Saxonberg
Associates

Published by
BookSumo, a division of Saxonberg
Associates
http://www.booksumo.com/

Stay To the End of the Cookbook and Receive....

I really appreciate when people, take the time to read all of my recipes.

So, as a gift for reading this entire cookbook you will receive a **massive collection of special recipes.**

Read to the end of and get my *Easy Specialty Cookbook Box Set for FREE*!

This box set includes the following:

1. *Easy Sushi Cookbook*

2. ***Easy Dump Dinner Cookbook***
3. ***Easy Beans Cookbook***

Remember this box set is about **EASY** cooking.

In the ***Easy Sushi Cookbook*** you will learn the easiest methods to prepare almost every type of Japanese Sushi i.e. *California Rolls, the Perfect Sushi Rice, Crab Rolls, Osaka Style Sushi*, and so many others.

Then we go on to *Dump Dinners*. Nothing can be easier than a Dump Dinner. In the ***Easy Dump Dinner Cookbook*** we will learn how to master our slow cookers and make some amazingly unique dinners that will take almost **no effort**.

Finally in the ***Easy Beans Cookbook*** we tackle one of my favorite side dishes: Beans. There are so many delicious ways to make Baked Beans and Bean Salads that I had to share them.

So stay till the end and then keep on cooking with my *Easy Specialty Cookbook Box Set*!

ABOUT THE AUTHOR.

Maggie Chow is the author and creator of your favorite *Easy Cookbooks* and *The Effortless Chef Series*. Maggie is a lover of all things related to food. Maggie loves nothing more than finding new recipes, trying them out, and then making them her own, by adding or removing ingredients, tweaking cooking times, and anything to make the recipe not only taste better, but be easier to cook!

For a complete listing of all my books please see my author page.

INTRODUCTION

Welcome to *The Effortless Chef Series*! Thank you for taking the time to download the *Easy Asian Cookbook*. Come take a journey with me into the delights of easy cooking. The point of this cookbook and all my cookbooks is to exemplify the effortless nature of cooking simply.

In this book we focus on the Asian world. You will find that even though the recipes are simple, the taste of the dishes is quite amazing.

So will you join me in an adventure of simple cooking? If the answer is yes (and I hope it is) please consult the table of contents to find the dishes you are most interested in. Once you are ready jump right in and start cooking.

— Chef Maggie Chow

TABLE OF CONTENTS

ANY ISSUES? CONTACT ME

If you find that something important to you is missing from this book please contact me at maggie@booksumo.com.

I will try my best to re-publish a revised copy taking your feedback into consideration and let you know when the book has been revised with you in mind.

:)

— Chef Maggie Chow

LEGAL NOTES

COMMON ABBREVIATIONS

cup(s)	C.
tablespoon	tbsp
teaspoon	tsp
ounce	oz.
pound	lb

*All units used are standard American measurements

CHAPTER 1: KOREAN

SPICY TOFU SALAD

Ingredients

- 3 green onions, chopped
- two tbsps. soy sauce
- two tbsps. toasted sesame seeds
- one half tsps. Korean chili pepper powder, or to taste
- one tsp. white sugar
- half tsp. toasted Asian sesame oil
- one half cups steamed Japanese rice
- half head of romaine lettuce (heart only), torn into bite-size pieces
- half cucumber - peeled, seeded, and chopped
- one (1 two ounce) package tofu, sliced

Directions

- Combine green onions, sesame seeds, Korean red pepper powder, soy sauce, sugar, and sesame oil in a regular sized bowl thoroughly
- Now put the rice in bowl and add a mixture of lettuce and cucumber before putting tofu over it.
- Now pour some sesame mixture over the tofu according to your tastes.

Amount per serving: (one large bowl)

Timing Information:

Preparation	Cooking	Total Time
10 mins		10 mins

Nutritional Information:

Calories	198 kcal
Carbohydrates	23.7 g
Cholesterol	0 mg
Fat	7.2 g
Fiber	1.9 g
Protein	10.4 g
Sodium	472 mg

* Percent Daily Values are based on a 2,000 calorie diet.

KIMCHEE SQUATS

Ingredients

- two lbs. chopped Chinese cabbage
- one tbsp. salt
- two tbsps. chopped green onion
- one clove garlic, crushed
- one tbsp. chili powder
- two tsps. minced fresh ginger root
- half cup light soy sauce
- half cup white wine vinegar
- two tsps. white sugar
- one dash sesame oil

Directions

- Let cabbage sit for 4 hours after adding some salt and massage it with your hands until you find that it is soft.
- Now drain all the liquid and add green onion, soy sauce, sugar, ginger, garlic and chili powder into this cabbage.
- Refrigerate for about 24 hours in a jar before serving.

Amount per serving: (6 total)

Timing Information:

Preparation	Cooking	Total Time
25 mins	10 mins	1 day 4 hrs 25 min

Nutritional Information:

Calories	36 kcal
Carbohydrates	6.8 g
Cholesterol	0 mg
Fat	0.5 g
Fiber	1.9 g
Protein	2.6 g
Sodium	1796 mg

* Percent Daily Values are based on a 2,000 calorie diet.

CARROT SALAD

Ingredients

- one lb. carrots, peeled and julienned (preferably with a mandolin)
- three cloves garlic, minced
- 1/4 cup vinegar
- one tbsp. white sugar
- two half tsps. salt
- 1/three cup vegetable oil
- half onion, minced
- one tsp. ground coriander
- half tsp. cayenne pepper

Directions

- Add garlic over carrots in a bowl and separately mix vinegar, sugar, and salt thoroughly.
- Cook onions in hot oil for about 5 minutes and add coriander and cayenne pepper before adding everything to the carrot mixture.
- Also add vinegar dressing over the mixture and refrigerate in a

sealed dish for about 24 hours while tossing it several times.

Amount per serving: (6 total)

Timing Information:

Preparation	Cooking	Total Time
30 mins	10 mins	1 hrs 30 mins

Nutritional Information:

Calories	119 kcal
Carbohydrates	8.9 g
Cholesterol	0 mg
Fat	9.3 g
Fiber	2 g
Protein	0.8 g
Sodium	767 mg

* Percent Daily Values are based on a 2,000 calorie diet.

Spicy Red Pepper Cucumbers

Ingredients

- one tsp. vegetable oil
- two tbsps. sesame seeds
- two tbsps. kochujang (Korean hot sauce)
- 1/4 cup white vinegar
- one tbsp. sesame oil
- 1 green onion, chopped
- one cucumber, halved, seeded and thinly sliced

Directions

- Place sesame seeds in a large bowl after cooking in hot vegetable oil for about three minutes and add kochujang, green onion and sesame oil into the sesame seeds.
- Now add cucumber and mix well.
- Serve.

Amount per serving: (2 total)

Timing Information:

Preparation	Cooking	Total Time
10 mins	5 mins	15 mins

Nutritional Information:

Calories	1092 kcal
Carbohydrates	57.5 g
Cholesterol	155 mg
Fat	78.6 g
Fiber	1.8 g
Protein	39.1 g
Sodium	2501 mg

* Percent Daily Values are based on a 2,000 calorie diet.

Salad with Sesame Dressing

Ingredients

- one head red leaf lettuce
- 4 green onions (white part only)
- 1/4 cup soy sauce
- 5 tbsps. water
- two tsps. white sugar
- 1/4 cup distilled white vinegar
- two tbsps. sesame oil
- one tbsp. red pepper flakes

Directions

- Place lettuce leaves into a bowl after washing and cutting.
- Now add the sliced white portion of your sliced green onions into the bowl containing the lettuce leaves.
- In a separate bowl mix soy sauce, white sugar, vinegar, sesame oil, water, and red pepper flakes and pour this mixture over the bowl containing lettuce leaves and green onions.
- Serve.

Amount per serving: (5 total)

Timing Information:

Preparation	Cooking	Total Time
10 mins		10 mins

Nutritional Information:

Calories	80 kcal
Carbohydrates	6.1 g
Cholesterol	0 mg
Fat	5.9 g
Fiber	1.6 g
Protein	2 g
Sodium	740 mg

* Percent Daily Values are based on a 2,000 calorie diet.

Korean Cucumber Salad

Ingredients

- three lbs. seedless cucumber, sliced paper-thin
- one half tbsps. sea salt
- half cup rice vinegar
- one tbsp. rice wine
- two tbsps. sesame oil
- two tbsps. honey
- two tbsps. freshly squeezed lemon juice
- 1 green onion, sliced
- one tbsp. toasted sesame seeds
- two walnut halves, finely chopped(optional)
- one clove garlic, minced
- one half tsps. Korean red pepper powder
- freshly ground black pepper to taste

Directions

- Drain liquid from cucumbers after putting some sea salt by letting it stand for about 15 minutes and wrapping it in a paper towel to get more water out of it.

- Now combine rice vinegar, rice wine, honey, green onion, sesame seeds, lemon juice, walnuts, garlic, sesame oil, Korean red pepper powder and ground black pepper in a medium sized bowl.
- In this mixture, add cucumbers and refrigerate for at least 30 minutes after wrapping with plastic paper.

Amount per serving: (10 total)

Timing Information:

Preparation	Cooking	Total Time
10 mins		40 mins

Nutritional Information:

Calories	117 kcal
Carbohydrates	15.8 g
Cholesterol	0 mg
Fat	6.1 g
Fiber	1.7 g
Protein	2.1 g
Sodium	1332 mg

* Percent Daily Values are based on a 2,000 calorie diet.

KIMCHEE JUN

(KIMCHEE PANCAKES)

Ingredients

- one cup kimchi, drained and chopped
- half cup reserved juice from kimchi
- one cup all-purpose flour
- two eggs
- 1 green onion, chopped
- one tbsp. vegetable oil
- salt to taste
- one tbsp. rice vinegar
- one tbsp. soy sauce
- half tsp. sesame oil
- half tsp. Korean chili pepper flakes (optional)
- half tsp. toasted sesame seeds (optional)

Directions

- Combine kimchi, flour, eggs, kimchi juice and green onion in a medium sized bowl.

- Cook pancakes made from ¼ cup of batter in hot vegetable oil for about 5 minutes each side.
- Now combine rice vinegar, sesame oil, chili pepper flakes, soy sauce and toasted sesame seeds in a bowl and serve this with pancakes.

Amount per serving: (8 total)

Timing Information:

Preparation	Cooking	Total Time
15 mins	15 mins	30 mins

Nutritional Information:

Calories	199 kcal
Carbohydrates	26.5 g
Cholesterol	93 mg
Fat	7.1 g
Fiber	1.6 g
Protein	7.4 g
Sodium	513 mg

* Percent Daily Values are based on a 2,000 calorie diet.

Jap Chae

(Glass Noodles)

Ingredients

- one pkg. (8 serving size) sweet potato vermicelli
- half cup reduced-sodium soy sauce
- 1/4 cup brown sugar
- half cup boiling water
- three tbsps. vegetable oil
- one tsp. toasted sesame seeds

Directions

- Cover the vermicelli with hot water after cutting it into small pieces for 10 minutes and add a mixture of soy sauce, boiling water, and brown sugar into it.
- Cook this mixture in hot oil for about 5 minutes and just before serving, add noodles over it.

Amount per serving: (4 total)

Timing Information:

Preparation	Cooking	Total Time
15 mins	5 mins	20 mins

Nutritional Information:

Calories	363 kcal
Carbohydrates	65.2 g
Cholesterol	0 mg
Fat	10.7 g
Fiber	0.6 g
Protein	1.9 g
Sodium	1073 mg

* Percent Daily Values are based on a 2,000 calorie diet.

Kongnamool

(Soybean Sprouts)

Ingredients

- one lb. soybean sprouts
- two tbsps. soy sauce
- 1/4 cup sesame oil
- two tbsps. Korean chili powder
- one half tsps. garlic, minced
- two tsps. sesame seeds
- 1/4 cup chopped green onion
- two tsps. rice wine vinegar, or to taste

Directions

- Cook bean sprouts in salty boiling water for about 15 seconds and drain the water.
- Put sprouts in ice cold water for about three minutes to stop the cooking process and when these bean sprouts are cold, set them aside.
- Now combine soy sauce, sesame seeds, sesame oil and chili

powder in a medium sized bowl and add bean sprouts to it.

- Now add some green onion and rice wine vinegar before refrigerating for some time.
- Serve

Amount per serving: (4 total)

Timing Information:

Preparation	Cooking	Total Time
10 mins	5 mins	15 mins

Nutritional Information:

Calories	376 kcal
Carbohydrates	21.4 g
Cholesterol	69 mg
Fat	21.9 g
Fiber	0.8 g
Protein	20.6 g
Sodium	1249 mg

* Percent Daily Values are based on a 2,000 calorie diet.

Zucchini In Korea

Ingredients

- 5 medium zucchini, sliced
- one bunch green onions, sliced
- 1/4 cup white vinegar
- half cup soy sauce
- 1/4 cup water
- two tbsps. sugar
- two tbsps. sesame oil
- ground black pepper to taste

Directions

- Mix zucchini, vinegar, soy sauce, water, sugar, green onions and sesame oil in a saucepan before adding pepper and cooking for about 20 minutes to get the zucchini tender.

Amount per serving: (6 total)

Timing Information:

Preparation	Cooking	Total Time
20 mins	20 mins	40 mins

Nutritional Information:

Calories	1092 kcal
Carbohydrates	57.5 g
Cholesterol	155 mg
Fat	78.6 g
Fiber	1.8 g
Protein	39.1 g
Sodium	2501 mg

* Percent Daily Values are based on a 2,000 calorie diet.

Korean Spicy Marinated Pork

(Korean Style Pork)

Ingredients

- 1/4 C. rice wine vinegar
- 2 tbsps soy sauce
- 1/2 C. gochujang (Korean hot pepper paste)
- 3 tbsps minced garlic
- 3 tbsps minced fresh ginger root
- 2 tbsps red pepper flakes
- 1/2 tsp black pepper
- 3 tbsps white sugar
- 3 green onions, cut into 2 inch pieces
- 1/2 yellow onion, cut into 1/4-inch thick rings
- 1 (2 lb) pork loin, cut into 1/4 inch slices
- 1/4 C. canola oil

Directions

Get a bowl, combine: yellow and
green onions, vinegar, sugar, soy
sauce, black pepper, pepper
paste, pepper flakes, ginger and
garlic.

Now add in the pieces of pork with
the mix and place a covering of
plastic around the dish.

Place everything in the fridge for 4
hrs.

Now stir fry your pork, in canola,
until fully done, for about 7 mins.

Cook the pork in batches.

Enjoy.

Amount per serving (8 total)

Timing Information:

Preparation	Cooking	Total Time
45 m	15 m	4 h

Nutritional Information:

Calories	300 kcal
Fat	17.3 g
Carbohydrates	16.8g
Protein	19.2 g
Cholesterol	55 mg
Sodium	390 mg

* Percent Daily Values are based on a 2,000 calorie diet.

Korean BBQ Short Ribs

Gal-Bi

(Korean Ribs)

Ingredients

- 3/4 C. soy sauce
- 3/4 C. water
- 3 tbsps white vinegar
- 1/4 C. dark brown sugar
- 2 tbsps white sugar
- 1 tbsp black pepper
- 2 tbsps sesame oil
- 1/4 C. minced garlic
- 1/2 large onion, minced
- 3 lbs Korean-style short ribs (beef chuck flanken, cut 1/3 to 1/2 inch thick across bones)

Directions

Get a bowl, combine: vinegar, water, soy sauce, onion, brown sugar,

garlic, regular sugar, sesame oil,
and regular pepper.
Add your ribs to this mix and cover
the bowl with some plastic.
Place the contents in the fridge
overnight.
Now grill the ribs for 6 mins per side
on an oiled grate.
Enjoy.

Amount per serving (5 total)

Timing Information:

Preparation	Cooking	Total Time
15 m	10 m	7 h 25 m

Nutritional Information:

Calories	710 kcal
Fat	55.5 g
Carbohydrates	23.2g
Protein	28.8 g
Cholesterol	112 mg
Sodium	2231 mg

* Percent Daily Values are based on a 2,000 calorie diet.

RED PEPPER POTATOES

Ingredients

- one half tbsps. soy sauce
- one pinch cayenne pepper, or to taste
- one half tbsps. vegetable oil
- three potatoes, cut into bite sized pieces
- 4 green onions, chopped
- one large red bell pepper, chopped
- two tsps. sesame seeds

Directions

- Mix cayenne pepper and soy sauce in a bowl and cook potatoes over hot vegetable oil for about 5 minutes or until golden.
- Continue to cook for another minute after adding onion bell pepper and sesame seeds.
- Add soy sauce mixture and cook for another 3 minutes.

Amount per serving: (4 total)

Timing Information:

Preparation	Cooking	Total Time
15 mins	20 mins	35 mins

Nutritional Information:

Calories	198 kcal
Carbohydrates	32.3 g
Cholesterol	0 mg
Fat	6.2 g
Fiber	5 g
Protein	4.6
Sodium	352 mg

* Percent Daily Values are based on a 2,000 calorie diet.

FIDDLEHEADS

Ingredients

- three cups fresh fiddlehead ferns, ends trimmed
- three tbsps. unfiltered extra-virgin olive oil
- one clove garlic, minced
- half tsp. sea salt
- half tsp. black pepper
- one tbsp. fresh lemon juice

Directions

- Cook fiddlehead ferns in salty boiling water for about 10 minutes and drain the water.
- Add pepper, and garlic in some hot olive oil along with the ferns for about 5 minutes and remove everything from the heat and add lemon juice before serving.

Amount per serving: (3 total)

Timing Information:

Preparation	Cooking	Total Time
15 mins	15 mins	30 mins

Nutritional Information:

Calories	376 kcal
Carbohydrates	21.4 g
Cholesterol	69 mg
Fat	21.9 g
Fiber	0.8 g
Protein	20.6 g
Sodium	1249 mg

* Percent Daily Values are based on a 2,000 calorie diet.

CRAB CAKES IN KOREA

Ingredients

- 1/4 cup mayonnaise
- two tbsps. chopped fresh cilantro
- one tbsp. chopped fresh ginger
- two tsps. Asian fish sauce (nuoc mam or nam pla)
- one (6 ounce) can crabmeat - drained, flaked and cartilage removed
- three ounces chopped shrimp
- one half cups fresh breadcrumbs, made from crustless French bread
- salt and pepper to taste
- one half tbsps. peanut oil

Directions

- Combine crab, shrimp, bread crumbs, fresh ginger, mayonnaise, fish sauce and cilantro together in a bowl before adding salt and pepper.
- Take one fourth of a cup of this mixture and place in a bowl

containing the remaining bread crumbs, and make a patty out of it.

- Do the same for the rest of the crab mixture.
- Now fry your patties in in hot oil over medium heat for about 5 minutes each side.
- Serve

Amount per serving: (4 total)

Timing Information:

Preparation	Cooking	Total Time
15 mins	35 mins	50 mins

Nutritional Information:

Calories	254 kcal
Carbohydrates	9.6 g
Cholesterol	75 mg
Fat	17.4 g
Fiber	0.5 g
Protein	14.5 g
Sodium	620 mg

* Percent Daily Values are based on a 2,000 calorie diet.

CORN AND CASHEW HUMMUS

Ingredients

- two cups corn kernels, thawed if frozen
- one cup cashews
- one tsp. lemon juice, or more to taste
- 1/4 tsp. salt
- 1/4 tsp. onion powder
- 1/4 tsp. garlic powder

Directions

- Place everything mentioned in a blender and blend it for about one minute.
- Serve with rice.

Amount per serving: (3 total)

Timing Information:

Preparation	Cooking	Total Time
5 mins		5 mins

Nutritional Information:

Calories	270 kcal
Carbohydrates	28.6 g
Cholesterol	0 mg
Fat	16.5 g
Fiber	3 g
Protein	7.8 g
Sodium	367 mg

* Percent Daily Values are based on a 2,000 calorie diet.

TOASTI

Ingredients

- half cup shredded cabbage
- half carrot, shredded
- one egg
- half tsp. soy sauce
- two tbsps. butter
- two slices bread, toasted

Directions

- Add egg and soy sauce into a mixture of cabbage and carrot, and mix thoroughly.
- Cook the patty made from this vegetable mixture in hot butter for about three minutes each side.
- Serve by placing contents between two slices of bread.

Amount per serving: (1 total)

Timing Information:

Preparation	Cooking	Total Time
10 mins	10 mins	20 mins

Nutritional Information:

Calories	431 kcal
Carbohydrates	30.9 g
Cholesterol	247 mg
Fat	29.8 g
Fiber	3 g
Protein	11.2 g
Sodium	751 mg

* Percent Daily Values are based on a 2,000 calorie diet.

Banana Waffles

Ingredients

- one 1/4 cups all-purpose flour
- three tsps. baking powder
- half tsp. salt
- one pinch ground nutmeg
- one cup 2% milk
- one egg
- two ripe bananas, sliced

Directions

- Combine nutmeg, baking powder, flour and salt and add milk and eggs.
- Pour two tbsps. of batter over preheated waffle iron after spraying the iron with non-stick cooking spray.
- Now place two slices of banana on the mixture pour another two tsps. of batter over these slices of banana.
- Cook for about three minutes or until golden brown.
- Serve.

Amount per serving: (4 total)

Timing Information:

Preparation	Cooking	Total Time
10 mins	30 mins	40 mins

Nutritional Information:

Calories	241 kcal
Carbohydrates	47.3 g
Cholesterol	50 mg
Fat	2.5 g
Fiber	2.6 g
Protein	8.3 g
Sodium	606 mg

* Percent Daily Values are based on a 2,000 calorie diet.

EGGS KIMCHI

Ingredients

- two tbsps. vegetable oil
- one cup kimchi, or to taste
- two large eggs, beaten

Directions

- Cook kimchi in hot oil over medium heat for about two minutes and add eggs, and cook for another three minutes to get the eggs tender.
- Serve.

Amount per serving: (4 total)

Timing Information:

Preparation	Cooking	Total Time
5 mins	5 mins	10 mins

Nutritional Information:

Calories	208 kcal
Carbohydrates	3.5 g
Cholesterol	186 mg
Fat	18.8 g
Fiber	0.9 g
Protein	7.5 g
Sodium	568 mg

* Percent Daily Values are based on a 2,000 calorie diet.

Seaweed Soup

Ingredients

- one (one ounce) package dried brown seaweed
- 1/4 lb. beef top sirloin, minced
- two tsps. sesame oil
- one half tbsps. soy sauce
- one tsp. salt, or to taste
- 6 cups water
- one tsp. minced garlic

Directions

- Cover seaweed with water to get them soft and cut them into two inch pieces.
- Cook beef, half tbsp. of soy sauce and some salt for about one minute in a saucepan over medium heat.
- Now add seaweed and the remaining soy sauce and cook for another minute while stirring continuously.

- Bring to boil after adding two cups of water and add garlic and the remaining water.
- Cook this for 20 minutes and add salt before serving.

Amount per serving: (4 total)

Timing Information:

Preparation	Cooking	Total Time
15 mins	30 mins	45 mins

Nutritional Information:

Calories	65 kcal
Carbohydrates	1 g
Cholesterol	17 mg
Fat	3.7 g
Fiber	0.1 g
Protein	6.8 g
Sodium	940 mg

* Percent Daily Values are based on a 2,000 calorie diet.

KIMCHEE JIGEH

(STEW)

Ingredients

- 6 cups water
- three cups napa cabbage Kim Chee, brine reserved
- two cups cubed fully cooked luncheon meat (e.g. Spam)
- three tbsps. chili powder
- salt, to taste
- ground black pepper, to taste

Directions

- Take a large saucepan and combine water, kim chee, spam, pepper, chili powder, kim chee brine and salt.
- Bring this mixture to boil and cook for about 20 minutes.
- Serve.

Amount per serving: (4 total)

Timing Information:

Preparation	Cooking	Total Time
5 mins	20 mins	25 mins

Nutritional Information:

Calories	303 kcal
Carbohydrates	10.6 g
Cholesterol	59 mg
Fat	24.1 g
Fiber	3.5 g
Protein	13.7 g
Sodium	2064 mg

* Percent Daily Values are based on a 2,000 calorie diet.

MISO

(BEAN CURD SOUP)

Ingredients

- three half cups water
- three tbsps. denjang (Korean bean curd paste)
- one tbsp. garlic paste
- half tbsp. dashi granules
- half tbsp. gochujang (Korean hot pepper paste)
- one zucchini, cubed
- one potato, peeled and cubed
- 1/4 lb. fresh mushrooms, quartered
- one onion, chopped
- one (1two ounce) package soft tofu, sliced

Directions

- Combine water, denjang, garlic paste, dashi and gochujang in saucepan over medium heat and let it boil for two minutes.

- Now add zucchini, potato, onions and mushrooms, and cook for another 7 minutes.
- Now add tofu and cook until tender.

Amount per serving: (4 total)

Timing Information:

Preparation	Cooking	Total Time
15 mins	20 mins	35 mins

Nutritional Information:

Calories	158 kcal
Carbohydrates	21.6 g
Cholesterol	0 mg
Fat	4.1 g
Fiber	3.4 g
Protein	9.1 g
Sodium	641 mg

* Percent Daily Values are based on a 2,000 calorie diet.

DOENJANG CHIGAE

(BEAN TOFU SOUP)

Ingredients

- three cups vegetable stock
- three cups water
- two cloves garlic, coarsely chopped
- two tbsps. Korean soy bean paste (doenjang)
- 4 green onions, chopped
- one zucchini, halved and cut into 1/2-inch slices
- half (16 ounce) package firm tofu, drained and cubed
- one jalapeno pepper, sliced

Directions

- Add garlic and soy bean paste into boiled vegetable stock stirring regularly to dissolve.
- Now add green onion, tofu, jalapeno and zucchini, and cook for 15 minutes at low heat.
- Serve.

Amount per serving: (6 total)

Timing Information:

Preparation	Cooking	Total Time
15 mins	25 mins	40 mins

Nutritional Information:

Calories	59 kcal
Carbohydrates	5 g
Cholesterol	0 mg
Fat	2.7 g
Fiber	1.6 g
Protein	4.9 g
Sodium	378 mg

* Percent Daily Values are based on a 2,000 calorie diet.

PINE NUT RICE SOUP

Ingredients

- one cup pine nuts
- two cups cooked long-grain white rice
- 6 cups water
- one tbsp. pine nuts
- one cup dates, pitted and chopped
- half tsp. white sugar
- salt to taste

Directions

- Blend rice, one cup pine nuts, and 2 glass of water in a blender.
- Add 4 cups of water and this pine nut mixture into saucepan, and bring it to boil.
- Cook for 10 minutes at low heat while stirring regularly to prevent it from burning.
- Garnish with sliced dates and more pine nuts.
- Serve.

Amount per serving: (6 total)

Timing Information:

Preparation	Cooking	Total Time
10 mins	10 mins	20 mins

Nutritional Information:

Calories	275 kcal
Carbohydrates	37 g
Cholesterol	0 mg
Fat	12.5 g
Fiber	3.3 g
Protein	7.8 g
Sodium	2 mg

* Percent Daily Values are based on a 2,000 calorie diet.

Shrimp Rice Soup

Ingredients

- two cups white rice
- 9 ounces shelled and deveined shrimp
- one tbsp. sesame oil
- one tbsp. rice wine
- 12 cups water
- salt to taste

Directions

- Let the rice stand for about two hours after rinsing it.
- Fry shrimp and rice wine in hot oil in a saucepan over medium heat and add rice cook for one minute.
- Pour some water into the saucepan and when the mixture is thick, turn the heat down to low and cook for another 10-15 minutes.
- Serve.

Amount per serving: (4 total)

Timing Information:

Preparation	Cooking	Total Time
2 hrs	20 mins	2 hrs 20 mins

Nutritional Information:

Calories	586 kcal
Carbohydrates	99.6 g
Cholesterol	128 mg
Fat	6.8 g
Fiber	1.6 g
Protein	25.9 g
Sodium	131 mg

* Percent Daily Values are based on a 2,000 calorie diet.

Seaweed Soup II

Ingredients

- one ounce dried wakame (brown) seaweed
- two tsps. sesame oil
- half cup extra-lean ground beef
- one tsp. salt, or to taste
- one half tbsps. soy sauce
- one tsp. minced garlic
- 7 cups water

Directions

- Let the seaweed stand in water for about 15 minutes to get soft, drain the water, and cut it into two inch pieces.
- Cook beef, 1/3 cup soy sauce and add some salt in hot oil in a saucepan over medium heat for about 4 minutes and add seaweed and the soy sauce that is left.
- Cook for another minute and add garlic and some water.

- Bring water to boil and lower the heat down to low and cook for another 15 minutes.
- Serve.

Amount per serving: (4 total)

Timing Information:

Preparation	Cooking	Total Time
10 mins	20 mins	40 mins

Nutritional Information:

Calories	376 kcal
Carbohydrates	21.4 g
Cholesterol	69 mg
Fat	21.9 g
Fiber	0.8 g
Protein	20.6 g
Sodium	1249 mg

* Percent Daily Values are based on a 2,000 calorie diet.

STEAK IN KOREA

Ingredients

- two lbs. thinly sliced Scotch fillet (chuck eye steaks)
- half cup soy sauce
- 5 tbsps. white sugar
- two half tbsps. sesame seeds
- two tbsps. sesame oil
- three shallots, thinly sliced
- two cloves garlic, crushed
- 5 tbsps. mirin (Japanese sweet wine)

Directions

- Combine soy sauce, sugar, sesame seeds, sesame oil, shallots, garlic, and mirin in a bowl before adding meat and mixing it thoroughly.
- Refrigerate for about 18 hours and fry this meat over hot oil for 10 minutes.
- Serve this meat with fried rice or salad.

Amount per serving: (6 total)

Timing Information:

Preparation	Cooking	Total Time
20 mins	10 mins	12 hrs 30 mins

Nutritional Information:

Calories	376 kcal
Carbohydrates	21.4 g
Cholesterol	69 mg
Fat	21.9 g
Fiber	0.8 g
Protein	20.6 g
Sodium	1249 mg

* Percent Daily Values are based on a 2,000 calorie diet.

BULGOGI

(KOREAN FLANK STEAK)

Ingredients

- 1 lb flank steak, thinly sliced
- 5 tbsps soy sauce
- 2 1/2 tbsps white sugar
- 1/4 C. diced green onion
- 2 tbsps minced garlic
- 2 tbsps sesame seeds
- 2 tbsps sesame oil
- 1/2 tsp ground black pepper

Directions

- Get a bowl, mix: black pepper, soy sauce, sesame oil, sugar, sesame seeds, garlic, and green onions.
- Add in your beef and place a covering of plastic around the bowl.

- Now place everything in the fridge for 60 mins.
- Grill your beef for 3 mins per side on an oiled grate.
- Enjoy.

Amount per serving (4 total)

Timing Information:

Preparation	Cooking	Total Time
10 m	5 m	1 h 15 m

Nutritional Information:

Calories	232 kcal
Fat	13.2 g
Carbohydrates	12.4g
Protein	16.2 g
Cholesterol	27 mg
Sodium	1157 mg

* Percent Daily Values are based on a 2,000 calorie diet.

Korean Marinade

Ingredients

- 1 C. white sugar
- 1 C. soy sauce
- 1 C. water
- 1 tsp onion powder
- 1 tsp ground ginger
- 1 tbsp lemon juice (optional)
- 4 tsps hot chili paste (optional)

Directions

- Get the following boiling in a big pot: ginger, sugar, onion powder, soy sauce, and water.
- Once it is all boiling set the heat to low and let the contents gently cook for 7 mins.
- Shut the heat and stir in the lemon juice and chili paste.
- Then add in your chicken and let it sit in the mix for at least 5 hrs before cooking.

NOTE: Your chicken can be grilled for the best tastes, or stir fried with medium heat.

Amount per serving (48 total)

Timing Information:

Preparation	Cooking	Total Time
10 m	15 m	25 m

Nutritional Information:

Calories	20 kcal
Fat	0.1 g
Carbohydrates	< 4.9g
Protein	0.3 g
Cholesterol	< 0 mg
Sodium	304 mg

* Percent Daily Values are based on a 2,000 calorie diet.

TAK TORITANG

(POTATO AND CHICKEN)

Ingredients

- 2 1/2 lbs chicken drumettes
- 2 large potatoes, cut into large chunks
- 2 carrots, cut into 2 inch pieces
- 1 large onion, cut into 8 pieces
- 4 cloves garlic, crushed
- 1/4 C. water
- 1/2 C. soy sauce
- 2 tbsps white sugar
- 3 tbsps hot pepper paste

Directions

- Get the following boiling in a big pot: hot pepper paste, potatoes, sugar, carrots, soy sauce, water, onions, and garlic.

- Once it is all boiling set the heat to its lowest level and cook the mix for 50 mins.
- At this point the liquid should be thick.
- Enjoy.

Amount per serving (4 total)

Timing Information:

Preparation	Cooking	Total Time
15 m	45 m	1 h

Nutritional Information:

Calories	447 kcal
Fat	14.1 g
Carbohydrates	54.7g
Protein	25.7 g
Cholesterol	60 mg
Sodium	1994 mg

* Percent Daily Values are based on a 2,000 calorie diet.

Pul-Kogi

(Beef BBQ II)

Ingredients

- 1 lb beef top sirloin, thinly sliced
- 6 cloves garlic, minced
- 1/2 pear - peeled, cored, and minced
- 2 green onions, thinly sliced
- 4 tbsps soy sauce
- 2 tbsps white sugar
- 1 tbsp sesame oil
- 1 tbsp rice wine
- 1 tbsp sesame seeds
- 1 tsp minced fresh ginger
- freshly ground black pepper to taste (optional)

Directions

- Get a bowl, combine: black pepper, garlic, ginger, pears, sesame seeds, green onions, soy

sauce, wine, sesame oil, and sugar.
- Add in your beef and stir.
- Place a covering of plastic on the bowl and place everything in the fridge for 4 hrs.
- Grab a broiler pan and coat it with oil.
- Now cook your beef under the broiler for 7 mins.
- Enjoy.

Amount per serving (4 total)

Timing Information:

Preparation	Cooking	Total Time
25 m	5 m	30 m

Nutritional Information:

Calories	276 kcal
Fat	14.9 g
Carbohydrates	13.8g
Protein	20.6 g
Cholesterol	60 mg
Sodium	947 mg

* Percent Daily Values are based on a 2,000 calorie diet.

KOREAN TERIYAKI

Ingredients

- 1/4 C. soy sauce
- 1 C. water
- 1/3 C. maple syrup
- 3 tbsps dark sesame oil
- 2 cloves garlic, crushed
- 1 tbsp minced fresh ginger root
- 2 tsps ground black pepper
- 5 skinless, boneless chicken breast halves
- 1 C. brown rice
- 2 C. water
- 2 tbsps cornstarch

Directions

- Get a bowl, combine: pepper, soy sauce, ginger, 1 C. of water, garlic, maple syrup, and sesame oil.
- Reserve 1/3 of a C. of the mix and then add in your chicken.

- Stir the chicken in the marinade and place a covering of plastic around the bowl.
- Put everything in the fridge for 3 hrs.
- Get your rice and 2 C. of water boiling.
- Once it is boiling, set the heat to its lowest level, place a lid on the pot, and let the rice cook for 50 mins.
- Coat a casserole dish with oil and then turn on your oven's broiler before doing anything else.
- Put your chicken pieces in the casserole dish and then begin to boil the associated marinade.
- Add in some cornstarch and stir the mix while it is boiling and continue heating until it is thick.
- At the same time cook your chicken for 9 mins each side under the broiler and baste the meat with the marinade.
- Enjoy.

Amount per serving (5 total)

Timing Information:

Preparation	Cooking	Total Time
15 m	1 h	3 h 15 m

Nutritional Information:

Calories	388 kcal
Fat	11.9 g
Carbohydrates	41.5g
Protein	27.7 g
Cholesterol	67 mg
Sodium	785 mg

* Percent Daily Values are based on a 2,000 calorie diet.

Bibimbap

(Vegetarian Approved)

Ingredients

- 2 tbsps sesame oil
- 1 C. carrot matchsticks
- 1 C. zucchini matchsticks
- 1/2 (14 oz.) can bean sprouts, drained
- 6 oz. canned bamboo shoots, drained
- 1 (4.5 oz.) can sliced mushrooms, drained
- 1/8 tsp salt to taste
- 2 C. cooked and cooled rice
- 1/3 C. sliced green onions
- 2 tbsps soy sauce
- 1/4 tsp ground black pepper
- 1 tbsp butter
- 3 eggs
- 3 tsps sweet red chili sauce, or to taste

Directions

- Stir fry your zucchini and carrots and in sesame oil for 7 mins then add in: mushrooms, bamboo, and sprouts.
- Stir fry the mix for 7 more mins then add in some salt and remove the veggies from the pan.
- Add in: black pepper, rice, soy sauce, and green onions. And get everything hot.
- Now in another pan fry your eggs in butter. When the yolks are somewhat runny but the egg whites are cooked place the eggs to the side. This should take about 3 mins of frying.
- Layer an egg on some rice.
- Add the veggies on top of the egg and some red chili sauce over everything.
- Enjoy.

Amount per serving (3 total)

Timing Information:

Preparation	Cooking	Total Time
30 m	20 m	50 m

Nutritional Information:

Calories	395 kcal
Fat	18.8 g
Carbohydrates	45g
Protein	13.6 g
Cholesterol	196 mg
Sodium	1086 mg

* Percent Daily Values are based on a 2,000 calorie diet.

KOREAN PORK DUMP DINNER

Ingredients

- 3 cloves garlic, pressed
- 1/2 C. chicken broth
- 1 tbsp Korean chili bean paste
- 1/2 C. soy sauce
- 6 pork chops
- salt and pepper to taste

Directions

- Add the following to your crock pot: soy sauce, garlic, bean paste, and chicken broth.
- Add some pepper and salt to your pork before adding it in as well.
- Stir everything in the slow cook before cooking the contents for 6 hrs with a low level of heat.
- Enjoy.

Amount per serving (6 total)

Timing Information:

Preparation	Cooking	Total Time
10 m	5 h	5 h 10 m

Nutritional Information:

Calories	142 kcal
Fat	6.7 g
Carbohydrates	3.5g
Protein	16 g
Cholesterol	39 mg
Sodium	1247 mg

* Percent Daily Values are based on a 2,000 calorie diet.

BULGOGI II

Ingredients

- 1/4 C. diced onion
- 5 tbsps soy sauce
- 2 1/2 tbsps brown sugar
- 2 tbsps minced garlic
- 2 tbsps sesame oil
- 1 tbsp sesame seeds
- 1/2 tsp cayenne
- salt and ground black pepper to taste
- 1 lb skinless, boneless chicken breasts, cut into thin strips

Directions

- Get a bowl, combine: black pepper, onions, salt, brown sugar, soy sauce, cayenne, garlic, sesame seeds, and sesame oils.
- Add in your chicken to the mix and stir the mix before pouring everything in a wok.

- Stir fry the contents until your chicken is fully done for about 17 mins.
- Enjoy.

Amount per serving (4 total)

Timing Information:

Preparation	Cooking	Total Time
15 m	15 m	30 m

Nutritional Information:

Calories	269 kcal
Fat	11.6 g
Carbohydrates	13.2g
Protein	27.5 g
Cholesterol	69 mg
Sodium	1230 mg

* Percent Daily Values are based on a 2,000 calorie diet.

CHICKEN FROM KOREA

Ingredients

- 1 (3 lb) whole chicken, meat remove from the bones, slices in the 1/8" thick square pieces
- 1/4 C. soy sauce
- 2 tbsps sesame seeds
- 1/8 tsp salt
- 1/8 tsp ground black pepper
- 1 green onion, minced
- 1 clove garlic, minced
- 1 tsp peanut oil
- 1 tbsp white sugar
- 1 tsp monosodium glutamate (MSG)

Directions

- Combine your cut chicken with some soy sauce in a bowl.
- Now toast your sesame seeds in a pan.

- Once they begin to pop place them in a bowl and top the seeds with salt.
- Now mash the seeds with a big wooden spoon and add in: MSG, pepper, sugar, onions, oil, and garlic.
- Now combine both bowls and let the chicken sit in the sesame mix for 35 mins.
- Begin to stir fry your chicken in the same pan for 2 mins before placing a cover on the pot and cooking until the meat is fully done.
- Enjoy.

Amount per serving (4 total)

Timing Information:

Preparation	Cooking	Total Time
10 m	40 m	50 m

Nutritional Information:

Calories	794 kcal
Fat	54.7 g
Carbohydrates	6g
Protein	65.3 g
Cholesterol	1255 mg
Sodium	1338 mg

* Percent Daily Values are based on a 2,000 calorie diet.

KOREAN STYLE VEGETABLES

Ingredients

- 5 medium zucchini, sliced
- 1 bunch green onions, sliced
- 1/4 C. white vinegar
- 1/2 C. soy sauce
- 1/4 C. water
- 2 tbsps sugar
- 2 tbsps sesame oil
- ground black pepper to taste

Directions

- Add the following to a big pot: sesame oil, zucchini, sugar, green onions, water, vinegar, and soy sauce.
- Add in some black pepper as well.
- Stir everything, then place a lid on the pot.
- Let the contents cook with a low level of heat for about 22 mins until the veggies are soft.

- Enjoy.

Amount per serving (6 total)

Timing Information:

Preparation	Cooking	Total Time
20 m	20 m	40 m

Nutritional Information:

Calories	106 kcal
Fat	4.9 g
Carbohydrates	14g
Protein	4 g
Cholesterol	0 mg
Sodium	1225 mg

* Percent Daily Values are based on a 2,000 calorie diet.

Soon Du Bu Jigae

(Tofu Stew)

Ingredients

- 1 tsp vegetable oil
- 1 tsp Korean chile powder
- 2 tbsps ground beef (optional)
- 1 tbsp Korean soy bean paste (doenjang)
- 1 C. water
- salt and pepper to taste
- 1 (12 oz.) package Korean soon tofu or soft tofu, drained and sliced
- 1 egg
- 1 tsp sesame seeds
- 1 green onion, diced

Directions

- Stir fry your beef and chili powder in veggie oil until the beef is fully done then add the bean paste and stir.

- Now add in the water and get everything boiling before adding in some pepper and salt.
- Once the mix is boiling add in your tofu and cook the contents for 4 mins.
- Shut the heat and crack your egg into the soup.
- Stir everything and let the egg poach before adding a garnishing of green onions and sesame seeds.
- Enjoy.

Amount per serving (2 total)

Timing Information:

Preparation	Cooking	Total Time
5 m	15 m	20 m

Nutritional Information:

Calories	242 kcal
Fat	16.5 g
Carbohydrates	7g
Protein	20 g
Cholesterol	99 mg
Sodium	415 mg

* Percent Daily Values are based on a 2,000 calorie diet.

KOREAN STYLE PIZZA

Ingredients

- 2 C. all-purpose flour
- 2 eggs
- 4 C. water
- 1/2 tsp salt
- 1 shallot, diced
- 1 green onion, diced
- 1/2 C. minced crabmeat
- 1/2 C. diced cooked pork
- 1/2 C. diced firm tofu
- 1 C. bean sprouts
- 1 C. frozen mixed vegetables, thawed
- 1/2 C. shredded cabbage
- 4 tsps canola oil
- 1/4 C. soy sauce
- 2 tbsps rice vinegar
- 1 tbsp sesame oil
- 1 chili pepper, diced (optional)

Directions

- Get a bowl, combine: chili pepper, soy sauce, sesame oil, and vinegar. Place this mix to the side.
- Get a 2nd bowl, combine: salt, flour, water, and eggs. Now add the: cabbage, crabmeat, mixed veggies, pork, sprouts, and tofu.
- Now it is important that you get your oil very in a skillet then add in enough of the batter to coat the bottom of the pan.
- Let this fry for 9 mins then flip it and cook for 4 more mins.
- Continue with all of the remaining mix.
- Finally top your dish with some of the sauce.
- Enjoy.

Amount per serving (8 total)

Timing Information:

Preparation	Cooking	Total Time
10 m	30 m	40 m

Nutritional Information:

Calories	233 kcal
Fat	7 g
Carbohydrates	30.1g
Protein	12.7 g
Cholesterol	63 mg
Sodium	663 mg

* Percent Daily Values are based on a 2,000 calorie diet.

CHOMPCHAE DEOPBAP

(TUNA AND RICE)

Ingredients

- 1 C. uncooked white rice
- 2 C. water
- 1 tbsp olive oil
- 3 cloves garlic, minced
- 1 (1/2 inch) piece fresh ginger, minced
- 1/2 onion, coarsely diced
- 1 C. kim chee
- 1/2 C. sliced cucumber
- 1/4 C. sliced carrots
- 2 tbsps soy sauce
- 2 tbsps rice vinegar
- salt and pepper to taste
- 1 tbsp Korean chili powder, or to taste
- 1 tbsp water, or as needed
- 1 (6 oz.) can tuna, drained

Directions

- Get your rice boiling with 2 C. of water, once it is boiling place a lid on the pot, set the heat to low, and let it cook for 23 mins.
- Stir fry your onions, ginger, and garlic in olive oil for 7 mins then add in: vinegar, carrots, soy sauce, pepper, salt, chili powder, cucumbers, and kimchee.
- Cook and add in your tuna, while stirring until everything is hot.
- Layer the rice with a topping of tuna mix on each plate.
- Enjoy.

Amount per serving (2 total)

Timing Information:

Preparation	Cooking	Total Time
10 m	40 m	50 m

Nutritional Information:

Calories	562 kcal
Fat	9 g
Carbohydrates	87.5g
Protein	31.8 g
Cholesterol	25 mg
Sodium	1507 mg

* Percent Daily Values are based on a 2,000 calorie diet.

KALBI JIM

(KOREAN RIBS II)

Ingredients

- 2 lbs beef short ribs, trimmed
- 1 green onion, diced
- 2 carrots, peeled and diced
- 4 cloves garlic, minced
- 1 (1 inch) piece fresh ginger root, diced
- 1/2 C. reduced-sodium soy sauce
- 1/4 C. brown sugar
- 2 C. water to cover

Directions

- Cut some incisions into your beef then add them into a pan with: brown sugar, green onions, soy sauce, carrots, ginger, and garlic.
- Add in some water to cover the contents and get everything boiling.

- Once it is all boiling set the heat to low and let the contents cook for 60 mins.
- Remove any excess oils then plate the contents.
- Enjoy.

Amount per serving (6 total)

Timing Information:

Preparation	Cooking	Total Time
20 m	1 h	1 h 20 m

Nutritional Information:

Calories	647 kcal
Fat	54.9 g
Carbohydrates	14.1g
Protein	23.3 g
Cholesterol	115 mg
Sodium	805 mg

* Percent Daily Values are based on a 2,000 calorie diet.

Korean Burrito

Ingredients

Meat:

- 6 cloves garlic, minced
- 2 tbsps Korean chili paste (gochujang)
- 1 tbsp soy sauce
- 2 tsps white sugar
- 1 tsp sesame oil
- 2 (10 oz.) cans chicken chunks, drained

Everything Else:

- 4 (10 inch) flour tortillas
- 2 tbsps vegetable oil
- 2 tsps butter, softened (optional)
- 1 C. fresh cilantro leaves
- 1/2 C. diced kimchi, squeezed dry (optional)
- 2 tbsps shredded sharp Cheddar cheese

- 1 tbsp salsa

Directions

- Set your oven to 350 degrees before doing anything else.
- Get a bowl, combine: sesame oil, garlic, sugar, soy sauce, and chili paste. Then add the chicken and stir everything.
- Cover your tortillas with some foil and cook them for 12 mins in the oven.
- At the same time begin to stir fry your chicken in veggie oil with the marinade.
- Cook the chicken for about 12 mins as well.
- Coat each tortilla with half a tsp of butter then add an equal amount of chicken to each.
- Add the following to each tortilla before folding: salsa, cilantro, cheddar, and kimchi.
- Shape everything into tacos and serve.

- Enjoy.

Amount per serving (4 total)

Timing Information:

Preparation	Cooking	Total Time
15 m	15 m	30 m

Nutritional Information:

Calories	597 kcal
Fat	29.1 g
Carbohydrates	45.6g
Protein	38.5 g
Cholesterol	97 mg
Sodium	1635 mg

* Percent Daily Values are based on a 2,000 calorie diet.

Korean Curry

Ingredients

- 1/4 C. olive oil, divided
- 1 1/2 lbs boneless pork chops, cut into cubes
- 1 large yellow onion, cut into cubes
- 2 large russet potatoes, peeled and cut into cubes
- 3 large carrots, peeled and cut into cubes
- 4 C. water
- 1 tbsp Korean-style curry powder (such as Assi(R) mild curry powder), or more to taste

Directions

- Stir fry your pork in 2 tbsps of olive oil for 8 mins.
- Then in another pot stir fry your carrots, potatoes, and onions in more olive oil for 8 mins.

- Add the pork to the veggies and add some water.
- Place a lid on the pot and let the contents gently boil for 22 mins.
- Shut the heat and add in your curry and stir everything until the spice is completely mixed in.
- Now cook everything for 25 more mins until the sauce is thick.
- Enjoy.

Amount per serving (6 total)

Timing Information:

Preparation	Cooking	Total Time
20 m	50 m	1 h 10 m

Nutritional Information:

Calories	303 kcal
Fat	13.6 g
Carbohydrates	27.9g
Protein	17.6 g
Cholesterol	36 mg
Sodium	60 mg

* Percent Daily Values are based on a 2,000 calorie diet.

Yaki Mandu

(Korean Egg Rolls)

Ingredients

- 1 lb ground beef
- 1 1/2 C. vegetable oil for frying
- 1/2 C. finely diced green onions
- 1/2 C. finely diced cabbage
- 1/2 C. finely diced carrot
- 1/2 C. minced garlic
- 4 tsps sesame oil, divided
- 1 tbsp toasted sesame seeds
- 1/2 tsp monosodium glutamate (such as Ac'cent(R))
- salt and ground black pepper to taste
- 2 eggs
- 1 (16 oz.) package wonton wrappers
- 3 tbsps soy sauce
- 2 tsps rice wine vinegar
- 1 tsp toasted sesame seeds, or more to taste

Directions

- Stir fry your beef for 8 mins.
- At the same time in another pot for 12 mins cook: ground beef, green onions, pepper, cabbage, salt, carrots, MSG, garlic, 1 tbsp of sesame oil and seeds. Then remove everything from the pan.
- Coat a wonton wrapper with some whisked egg and then add 1 tsp of beef mix into it.
- Then fold everything into a triangle and crimp the edges.
- Do this for all your ingredients.
- Then for 3 mins per side fry the wontons then place layer them on some paper towels.
- Get a bowl, combine: 1 tsp sesame seeds, soy sauce, 1 tsp sesame oil, and vinegar.
- Use this as topping for your wontons.
- Enjoy.

Amount per serving (25 total)

Timing Information:

Preparation	Cooking	Total Time
30 m	15 m	45 m

Nutritional Information:

Calories	125 kcal
Fat	5.8 g
Carbohydrates	12.1g
Protein	5.7 g
Cholesterol	28 mg
Sodium	246 mg

* Percent Daily Values are based on a 2,000 calorie diet.

CHICKEN STEW

Ingredients

- 1 1/2 C. water
- 1/4 C. soy sauce
- 2 tbsps rice wine
- 2 tbsps Korean red chili pepper paste (gochujang)
- 2 tbsps Korean red chili pepper flakes (gochugaru)
- 1 tbsp honey
- 1 tbsp white sugar
- 1 pinch ground black pepper
- 3 lbs bone-in chicken pieces, trimmed of fat and cut into small pieces
- 10 oz. potatoes, cut into large chunks
- 2 carrots, cut into large chunks
- 1/2 large onion, cut into large chunks
- 4 large garlic cloves, or more to taste

- 2 slices fresh ginger, or more to taste
- 2 scallions, cut into 2-inch lengths
- 1 tbsp sesame oil
- 1 tsp sesame seeds

Directions

- Get the following boiling in a big pot: chicken, water, black pepper, soy sauce, sugar, wine, honey, pepper paste, and pepper flakes.
- Once everything is boiling set the heat to low and place a lid on the pot.
- Let the contents cook for 17 mins.
- Add in: ginger, potatoes, garlic, carrots, and onions and cook the mix for 17 more mins.
- Take off the lid and continue cooking for 12 more mins.
- Now add in some sesame seeds, scallions, and sesame oil.
- Enjoy.

Amount per serving (4 total)

Timing Information:

Preparation	Cooking	Total Time
20 m	45 m	1 h 5 m

Nutritional Information:

Calories	896 kcal
Fat	69.1 g
Carbohydrates	136.1g
Protein	33.4 g
Cholesterol	121 mg
Sodium	1111 mg

* Percent Daily Values are based on a 2,000 calorie diet.

KIMCHI

(VEGETARIAN APPROVED)

Ingredients

- 1 head Napa cabbage, cubed
- 1/4 C. salt, divided
- 6 cloves garlic
- 1 (1 inch) piece fresh ginger root, peeled and diced
- 1 small white onion, peeled and diced
- 2 tbsps water
- 3 green onions, minced
- cayenne pepper to taste
- 1 ripe persimmon, diced
- 1 small radish, shredded
- 1 cucumber, diced (optional)

Directions

- Get a bowl and combine your cabbage and salt.

- Let it sit for 60 mins then add in more salt and let it stand for 60 more mins.
- Now remove all the liquids and wash the leaves off.
- Now blend the following until paste-like: onions, ginger, and garlic.
- Add this to the cabbage along with: cucumbers, green onions, persimmon, cayenne, and radishes.
- Place a covering on the bowl and let it sit in the fridge for at least 2 days.
- Enjoy.

Amount per serving (30 total)

Timing Information:

Preparation	Cooking	Total Time
25 m		3 d 2 h 25 m

Nutritional Information:

Calories	6 kcal
Fat	< 0 g
Carbohydrates	< 1.5g
Protein	< 0.3 g
Cholesterol	< 0 mg
Sodium	932 mg

* Percent Daily Values are based on a 2,000 calorie diet.

EGG ROLLS

Ingredients

- 1/2 (8 oz.) package dry thin Asian rice noodles (rice vermicelli)
- 1/2 medium head cabbage, cored and shredded
- 1 (12 oz.) package firm tofu
- 2 small zucchini, shredded
- 4 green onions, finely diced
- 4 cloves garlic, finely diced
- 1 tbsp ground black pepper
- 2 tbsps Asian (toasted) sesame oil
- 2 eggs, slightly beaten
- 2 tsps salt
- 1 (12 oz.) package round wonton wrappers
- 1/2 C. vegetable oil for frying

Directions

- Boil your noodles in water for 6 mins. Then remove all the liquids and run them under cold water.

- Now dice the noodles and place everything to the side.
- Squeeze your cabbage to drain any liquids and place them in a bowl with: noodles, tofu, salt, zucchini, eggs, sesame oil, green onions, black pepper, and garlic.
- Mix everything with your hands and try to break up your tofu pieces.
- Add two tsp of mix into your wonton wrappers and coat the edge with some water before shaping the wrapper into a triangle and crimping the edges.
- Continue for all your ingredients then fry the wontons in veggie oil for 4 mins per side.
- Enjoy.

Amount per serving (6 total)

Timing Information:

Preparation	Cooking	Total Time
45 m	15 m	1 h

Nutritional Information:

Calories	534 kcal
Fat	28.4 g
Carbohydrates	56.9g
Protein	14.6 g
Cholesterol	67 mg
Sodium	1177 mg

* Percent Daily Values are based on a 2,000 calorie diet.

KOREAN SUSHI

Ingredients

- 1 C. uncooked glutinous white rice (sushi rice)
- 1 1/2 C. water
- 1 tbsp sesame oil
- salt, to taste
- 2 eggs, beaten
- 4 sheets sushi nori (dry seaweed)
- 1 cucumber, cut into thin strips
- 1 carrot, cut into thin strips
- 4 slices American processed cheese, cut into thin strips
- 4 slices cooked ham, cut into thin strips
- 2 tsps sesame oil

Directions

- Get your water and rice boiling.
- Once it is boiling, place a lid on the pot, and set the heat to low.
- Let the rice cook for 15 mins.

- Now pour the rice into a casserole dish to lose its heat.
- At same time as the rice is cooking fry your eggs without stirring.
- Place your nori sheet on a counter top and layer each with an equal amount of rice.
- Now layer: ham, egg, cucumbers, cheese, and carrots.
- Roll up the sheet with a bamboo mat and top each with half a tsp of sesame oil.
- Dice up the roll into 6 pieces of sushi.
- Enjoy.

Amount per serving (4 total)

Timing Information:

Preparation	Cooking	Total Time
40 m	20 m	1 h

Nutritional Information:

Calories	354 kcal
Fat	15.2 g
Carbohydrates	41.2g
Protein	11.9 g
Cholesterol	113 mg
Sodium	510 mg

* Percent Daily Values are based on a 2,000 calorie diet.

CHAP CHEE NOODLES

Ingredients

- 1 tbsp soy sauce
- 1 tbsp sesame oil
- 2 green onions, finely diced
- 1 clove garlic, minced
- 1 tsp sesame seeds
- 1 tsp sugar
- 1/4 tsp black pepper
- 1/3 lb beef top sirloin, thinly sliced
- 2 tbsps vegetable oil
- 1/2 C. thinly sliced carrots
- 1/2 C. sliced bamboo shoots, drained
- 1/4 lb napa cabbage, sliced
- 2 C. diced fresh spinach
- 3 oz. cellophane noodles, soaked in warm water
- 2 tbsps soy sauce
- 1 tbsp sugar
- 1/2 tsp salt
- 1/4 tsp black pepper

Directions

- Get a bowl, combine: a quarter of a C. of pepper, 1 tbsp of soy sauce, 1 tsp of sugar, sesame oil, sesame seeds, garlic, and green onions. Add in the beef and let the content sit for 17 mins.
- Now stir fry the beef in oil until fill done then add in: spinach, carrots, cabbage, and bamboo. Cook for 2 more mins before add in: quarter tsp of pepper, half a tsp salt, 1 tbsps sugar, 2 tbsps of soy sauce, and noodles.
- Set the heat to low and heat all the contents up.
- Enjoy.

Amount per serving (4 total)

Timing Information:

Preparation	Cooking	Total Time
35 m	20 m	55 m

Nutritional Information:

Calories	264 kcal
Fat	12.5 g
Carbohydrates	27.9g
Protein	10.6 g
Cholesterol	23 mg
Sodium	1025 mg

* Percent Daily Values are based on a 2,000 calorie diet.

GALBI

(KOREAN SHORT RIBS III)

Ingredients

- 5 lbs beef short ribs, cut flanken style
- 5 cloves garlic
- 1 onion, coarsely diced
- 1 Asian pear, cored and cubed
- 1 C. soy sauce (such as Kikkoman(R))
- 1 C. brown sugar
- 1/4 C. honey
- 1/4 C. sesame oil
- black pepper to taste

Directions

- Submerge your ribs in water for 60 mins then then drain them.
- Puree the following in a blender: pear, onions, and garlic. Add this to a bowl with: black pepper, soy

sauce, sesame oil, brown sugar, and honey. Place your ribs in the mix and let it sit in the fridge for 8 hrs with a covering of plastic.

- Now grill your beef on an oiled grate for 7 mins per side.
- Enjoy.

Amount per serving (6 total)

Timing Information:

Preparation	Cooking	Total Time
1 h 30 m	10 m	9 h 40 m

Nutritional Information:

Calories	1092 kcal
Fat	78.6 g
Carbohydrates	157.5g
Protein	39.1 g
Cholesterol	155 mg
Sodium	2501 mg

* Percent Daily Values are based on a 2,000 calorie diet.

CHAPTER 2: JAPANESE

OKONOMIYAKI

(VARIETY PANCAKE)

(お好み焼き)

Ingredients

- 12 ounces sliced bacon
- 1 1/3 cups water
- 4 eggs
- 3 cups all-purpose flour
- 1 tsp salt
- 1 medium head cabbage, cored and sliced
- 2 tbsps minced pickled ginger
- 1/4 cup tonkatsu sauce or barbeque sauce

Directions

- Get a frying pan. Bacon should be fried with a medium heat. Soak excess oils with paper towel and put to the side.

- Get a bowl. Combine some water and eggs. Next combine in slowly, your flour, and then add salt.
- Combine with the flour: the ginger, and cabbage and mix until even.
- Get a 2nd frying pan or use the one from earlier. Add some nonstick spray to it. Take 1 / 4 cup of batter and put it in the middle of the pan.
- Cover the batter with 4 bacon strips. Make sure the batter is circular. Fry for 6 mins. Turn over the batter and cook the opposite side until golden. Set aside.
- Garnish with tonkatsu sauce. Cook all the batter in the same manner.
- Enjoy.

Servings: 4 servings

Timing Information:

Preparation	Cooking	Total Time
15 mins	30 mins	45 mins

Nutritional Information:

Calories	659 kcal
Carbohydrates	90.7 g
Cholesterol	217 mg
Fat	19.4 g
Fiber	8.3 g
Protein	29.3 g
Sodium	1531 mg

* Percent Daily Values are based on a 2,000 calorie diet.

CHICKEN WINGS IN JAPAN

(鶏手羽肉)

Ingredients

- 3 pounds chicken wings
- 1 egg, lightly beaten
- 1 cup all-purpose flour for coating
- 1 cup butter

SAUCE

- 3 tbsps soy sauce
- 3 tbsps water
- 1 cup white sugar
- 1/2 cup white vinegar
- 1/2 tsp garlic powder, or to taste
- 1 tsp salt

Directions

- Get your oven to 350 degrees before doing anything else.
- Slice your wings into two pieces. Get two bowls: one with egg, another with flour.

- Coat the wings with egg first, then flour.
- Get a frying pan and get butter melted.
- Fry wings until completely golden brown.
- Then move the wings into a saucepan.
- Get a bowl mix the following: salt, soy sauce, garlic powder, water, vinegar, and sugar. Use to coat wings.
- Enter wings into the oven for 40 mins. Make sure to baste with remaining wet mixture occasionally.
- Enjoy.

Servings: 6 servings

Timing Information:

Preparation	Cooking	Total Time
15 mins	45 mins	1 hr

Nutritional Information:

Calories	675 kcal
Carbohydrates	51.4 g
Cholesterol	158 mg
Fat	44.3 g
Fiber	0.7 g
Protein	18.9 g
Sodium	1112 mg

- Percent Daily Values are based on a 2,000 calorie diet.

ZUCCHINI STIR FRY

(ズッキーニと玉ねぎ)

Ingredients

- 2 tbsps vegetable oil
- 1 medium onion, thinly sliced
- 2 medium zucchinis, cut into thin strips
- 2 tbsps teriyaki sauce
- 1 tbsp soy sauce
- 1 tbsp toasted sesame seeds
- ground black pepper

Directions

- Get a frying pan hot with oil. For 5 mins stir fry onions.
- Add and stir-fry zucchini for an additional min.
- Combine into the zucchini your sesame seeds, teriyaki sauce, and soy sauce. Fry for 5 mins.
- Finally add pepper.
- Enjoy.

Servings: 4 servings

Timing Information:

Preparation	Cooking	Total Time
10 mins	10 mins	20 mins

Nutritional Information:

Calories	110 kcal
Carbohydrates	8.1 g
Cholesterol	0 mg
Fat	8.2 g
Fiber	1.9 g
Protein	2.7 g
Sodium	581 mg

* Percent Daily Values are based on a 2,000 calorie diet.

The Easiest Japanese Fruit Pie

(フルーツパイ)

Ingredients

- 1 (9 inch) unbaked pie shell
- 2 eggs, beaten
- 1/3 cup butter, melted
- 1 cup white sugar
- 1 tsp vanilla extract
- 1 tbsp distilled white vinegar
- 1/2 cup chopped pecans
- 1/2 cup shredded coconut
- 1/2 cup raisins

Directions

- Get your oven hot to 350 degrees.
- Get a bowl. Mix together until even and smooth: vinegar, eggs, sugar and butter.
- Mix in raisins, pecans, and coconut. Put everything in a pie crust.
- Bake for 40 mins.

- Enjoy.

Servings: 1 pie

Timing Information:

Preparation	Cooking	Total Time
10 mins	40 mins	50 mins

Nutritional Information:

Calories	404 kcal
Carbohydrates	47.7 g
Cholesterol	67 mg
Fat	23.1 g
Fiber	1.7 g
Protein	3.8 g
Sodium	243 mg

* Percent Daily Values are based on a 2,000 calorie diet.

BEEF STIR-FRY

(牛肉の炒め)

Ingredients

- 2 pounds boneless beef sirloin or beef top round steaks (3/4" thick)
- 3 tbsps cornstarch
- 1 (10.5 ounce) can Campbell's® Condensed Beef Broth
- 1/2 cup soy sauce
- 2 tbsps sugar
- 2 tbsps vegetable oil
- 4 cups sliced shiitake mushrooms
- 1 head Chinese cabbage (bok choy), thinly sliced
- 2 medium red peppers, cut into 2"-long strips
- 3 stalks celery, sliced
- 2 medium green onions, cut into 2" pieces
- Hot cooked regular long-grain white rice

Directions

- To start this recipe grab a knife and begin to cut your beef into some thin long strips.
- Grab a medium sized bowl and combine the following ingredients: sugar, broth, soy, and cornstarch.
- After combining the ingredients set them aside.
- Get your wok hot over a high level of heat and add one 1 tbsp of oil to it.
- Once your oil is hot combine the following ingredients in it: green onions, mushrooms, celery, cabbage, and peppers.
- Fry these veggies down until you find that they are soft. Set aside.
- Now grab your cornstarch mixture and put it in the pot. Stir-fry until you find that it has thickened.
- Once thick, combine the cornstarch with your beef and veggies.
- Fry until beef is cooked completely.
- Let contents cool.
- Enjoy.

Servings: 8 servings

Timing Information:

Preparation	Cooking	Total Time
30 mins	15 mins	45 mins

Nutritional Information:

Calories	290 kcal
Carbohydrates	26.4 g
Cholesterol	39 mg
Fat	7.6 g
Fiber	2.6 g
Protein	26.4 g
Sodium	1271 mg

* Percent Daily Values are based on a 2,000 calorie diet.

TOFU MUSHROOM SOUP

(豆腐のキノコのスープ)

Ingredients

- 3 cups prepared dashi stock
- 1/4 cup sliced shiitake mushrooms
- 1 tbsp miso paste
- 1 tbsp soy sauce
- 1/8 cup cubed soft tofu
- 1 green onion, diced

Directions

- Get a saucepan. Add your stock, get it boiling. Once boiling add mushrooms and cook for 4 mins.
- Get a bowl. Combine soy sauce and miso paste evenly. Mix this with your stock.
- For 6 mins let broth cook. Add some diced green onion.
- Enjoy.

Servings: 2 servings

Timing Information:

Preparation	Cooking	Total Time
10 mins	10 mins	20 mins

Nutritional Information:

Calories	100 kcal
Carbohydrates	4.8 g
Cholesterol	3 mg
Fat	3.9 g
Fiber	1 g
Protein	11 g
Sodium	1326 mg

* Percent Daily Values are based on a 2,000 calorie diet.

UDON SOUP

(うどんスープ)

Ingredients

- 6 cups prepared dashi stock
- 1/4 pound chicken, cut into chunks
- 2 carrots, diced
- 1/3 cup soy sauce
- 3 tbsps mirin
- 1/2 tsp white sugar
- 1/3 tsp salt
- 2 (12 ounce) packages firm tofu, cubed
- 1/3 pound shiitake mushrooms, sliced
- 5 ribs and leaves of bok choy, diced
- 1 (9 ounce) package fresh udon noodles
- 4 eggs
- 2 leeks, diced

Directions

- Get a sauce pan. Heat the following: salt, dashi stock, sugar, carrots, mirin, chicken, and soy sauce. Allow everything to lightly boil until your chicken is cooked fully (8 mins).
- Mix in some bok choy, mushrooms, and tofu. Let everything continue simmering for 6 mins.
- Add your noodles and cook for 5 more mins. Finally add leeks.
- Take your eggs and crack them over the soup. Let the soup cook for 5 mins until eggs are done.
- Enjoy.

Servings: 4 servings

Timing Information:

Preparation	Cooking	Total Time
15 mins	25 mins	40 mins

Nutritional Information:

Calories	548 kcal
Carbohydrates	53.4 g
Cholesterol	206 mg
Fat	17.2 g
Fiber	2.8 g
Protein	42.2 g
Sodium	2491 mg

* Percent Daily Values are based on a 2,000 calorie diet.

JAPANESE SALAD DRESSING

(サラダドレッシング)

Ingredients

- 2 tbsps minced fresh ginger root
- 1/3 cup minced onion
- 1/4 cup minced celery
- 1/4 cup low-sodium soy sauce
- 1/2 lime, juiced
- 1 tbsp white sugar
- 1 tbsp ketchup
- 1/4 tsp ground black pepper
- 1/2 cup vegetable oil

Directions

- Get a food processor. Process the following: celery, onion, and ginger until smooth.
- Mix in the following with your celery: pepper, soy sauce, ketchup, sugar and lime juice. Process for 30 secs until smooth.

- Continually run the processor while adding oil until everything becomes dressing-like.
- Enjoy.

Servings: 1 1/4 cup

Timing Information:

Preparation	Cooking	Total Time
15 mins		15 mins

Nutritional Information:

Calories	220 kcal
Carbohydrates	6.3 g
Cholesterol	0 mg
Fat	21.9 g
Fiber	0.5 g
Protein	0.9 g
Sodium	464 mg

* Percent Daily Values are based on a 2,000 calorie diet.

DEVILED EGGS JAPANESE STYLE

(デビルド卵)

Ingredients

- 9 eggs
- 2 tbsps sesame seeds
- 1/2 cup mayonnaise
- 2 tsps soy sauce
- 2 tsps wasabi paste
- 2 tsps rice wine vinegar
- 2 tbsps thinly sliced green onions
- 4 tbsps panko bread crumbs

Directions

- Boil your eggs in a saucepan. Once the water is boiling let it continue about 10 to 15 mins. Drain the water and run cold water over your eggs.
- Remove the shells. Place the eggs to the side.
- Get a frying pan and fry some sesame seeds for 4 mins. Set seeds aside.

- Split your shelled eggs and remove the yolks.
- Get your food processor and process the following until smooth: egg yolks, rice vinegar, mayo, wasabi paste and soy sauce.
- Put in some bread crumbs and green onion and pulse it a few more times.
- Put the processed contents into the center of your eggs and garnish each egg with sesame seeds.
- Enjoy.

Servings: 18 deviled eggs

Timing Information:

Preparation	Cooking	Total Time
35 mins	20 mins	55 mins

Nutritional Information:

Calories	91 kcal
Carbohydrates	2.1 g
Cholesterol	95 mg
Fat	7.9 g
Fiber	0.1 g
Protein	3.6 g
Sodium	122 mg

* Percent Daily Values are based on a 2,000 calorie diet.

JAPANESE RICE AND EGGS

(ご飯と卵)

Ingredients

- 1 cup cooked white or brown rice
- 2 thin slices cooked ham, cubed
- 2 tbsps ketchup
- 1 slice processed cheese food (such as Velveeta ®) (optional)
- 2 eggs
- salt and pepper to taste
- 1 tbsp ketchup
- 1/4 tsp chopped fresh parsley

Directions

- Get a frying pan, add nonstick spray. Combine your ham, cheese, 2 tbsps of ketchup, and cooked rice in the pan. Fry for about 9 mins.
- Put everything in a bowl or container.
- Get another bowl and whisk pepper, salt and eggs together.

- Get another frying pan and use some nonstick spray. Pour in eggs. As the edge of the egg cooks you should lift it. So the uncooked portion runs underneath. Do this until everything is fully cooked. Turn off the stove.
- Fold egg into a semi-circle and place on top of the rice.
- You can also add a tbsp of ketchup and parsley for a garnish.
- Enjoy.

Servings: 1 serving

Timing Information:

Preparation	Cooking	Total Time
5 mins	15 mins	20 mins

Nutritional Information:

Calories	521 kcal
Carbohydrates	59.3 g
Cholesterol	403 mg
Fat	20.2 g
Fiber	0.8 g
Protein	26.7 g
Sodium	1300 mg

* Percent Daily Values are based on a 2,000 calorie diet.

MACKEREL

(マックワイヤー)

Ingredients

- 4 mackerel fillets
- 1/4 cup soy sauce
- 1/4 cup mirin (Japanese sweet wine)
- 1 tbsp white sugar
- 1/2 tbsp grated fresh ginger root

Directions

- Clean your fish with cold water and remove any excess water with paper towels.
- Get a bowl and combine the following evenly: ginger, soy sauce, sugar, and mirin. Use as a marinade for your fish. Place a lid on the bowl. Chill contents for 25 mins.
- Turn on your broiler and get it hot, a grill could be used also.

- Place fillets under the broiler for 9 mins. Try to baste the fish a few times throughout the cooking time.
- Drizzle with lemon juice or radish.
- Enjoy.

Servings: 4 servings

Timing Information:

Preparation	Cooking	Total Time
20 mins	8 mins	28 mins

Nutritional Information:

Calories	234 kcal
Carbohydrates	9.2 g
Cholesterol	53 mg
Fat	9 g
Fiber	0.1 g
Protein	23.9 g
Sodium	1000 mg

* Percent Daily Values are based on a 2,000 calorie diet.

TOFU BURGER

(デッドバーガー)

Ingredients

- 1 (14 ounce) package firm tofu
- 1 pound ground beef
- 1/2 cup sliced shiitake mushrooms
- 2 tbsps miso paste
- 1 egg, lightly beaten
- 1 tsp salt
- 1 tsp ground black pepper
- 1/4 tsp ground nutmeg
- 1/4 cup mirin (Japanese sweet wine)
- 2 tbsps soy sauce
- 1 tsp garlic paste
- 1/4 tsp minced fresh ginger root
- 1 tbsp vegetable oil

Directions

- Remove excess liquid from your tofu. By placing it between two plates for 20 mins. Using something heavy on top to apply a constant downward force.

- Dice tofu into cubes.
- Get a bowl and mix the following: nutmeg, tofu, pepper, shiitake, salt, miso paste, and egg. Form 6 balls from this mixture and shape them into burgers.
- Get another bowl and mix the following: ginger, mirin, garlic paste, and soy sauce. Put to the side.
- Get a frying pan. Heat veggie oil.
- Fry burgers for 2 mins each side. Set heat to low. Place a lid on the pan.
- Let the burgers lightly fry for 5 mins.
- Remove excess oils. Then cover the burgers with the wet mixture of soy sauce. Coat both sides of the burgers by turning them over.
- Enjoy.

Servings: 6 servings

Timing Information:

Preparation	Cooking	Total Time
25 mins	20 mins	45 mins

Nutritional Information:

Calories	307 kcal
Carbohydrates	8.9 g
Cholesterol	77 mg
Fat	18.1 g
Fiber	2.1 g
Protein	25.5 g
Sodium	999 mg

* Percent Daily Values are based on a 2,000 calorie diet.

Maggie's Favorite Mushrooms

(キノコ)

Ingredients

- 4 Portobello mushroom caps
- 3 tbsps soy sauce
- 2 tbsps sesame oil
- 1 tbsp minced fresh ginger root
- 1 small clove garlic, minced

Directions

- Set your broiler to low. The rack should be placed 6 inches from the heating source (ideally).
- Run mushrooms under cold water until clean. Place mushrooms with the top's down on the baking sheet.
- Get a bowl mix the following evenly: sesame oil, garlic, soy sauce, and ginger. Cover the tops of the mushrooms with it.
- Cook mushrooms for 10 mins.

- Enjoy.

Servings: 2 servings

Timing Information:

Preparation	Cooking	Total Time
5 mins	10 mins	15 mins

Nutritional Information:

Calories	196 kcal
Carbohydrates	14.2 g
Cholesterol	0 mg
Fat	14.1 g
Fiber	3.6 g
Protein	7.3 g
Sodium	1367 mg

* Percent Daily Values are based on a 2,000 calorie diet.

CUCUMBER SALAD IN JAPAN

(キュウリのサラダ)

Ingredients

- 2 tbsps white sugar
- 2 tbsps rice vinegar
- 1 tsp Asian (toasted) sesame oil
- 1 tsp chili paste (sambal oelek)
- salt to taste
- 2 large cucumbers - peeled, seeded, and cut into 1/4-inch slices

Directions

- Get a bowl. Mix the following evenly: salt, sugar, chili paste, sesame oil, and rice vinegar.
- Combine with the wet mixture, your cucumbers, and set the salad to marinade for 35 mins on a countertop.
- Enjoy the salad at room temp.

Servings: 4 servings

Timing Information:

Preparation	Cooking	Total Time
15 mins		45 mins

Nutritional Information:

Calories	55 kcal
Carbohydrates	10.5 g
Cholesterol	0 mg
Fat	1.6 g
Fiber	1 g
Protein	0.8 g
Sodium	111 mg

* Percent Daily Values are based on a 2,000 calorie diet.

PORK LOIN AND GINGER

(ジンジャーポーク)

Ingredients

- 1 tbsp grated fresh ginger root
- 2 tbsps soy sauce
- 2 tbsps sake
- 2 tbsps mirin
- 1 pound thinly sliced pork loin
- 3 tbsps vegetable oil

Directions

- Get a bowl. Combine the following: mirin, ginger, sake, and soy sauce. Use this as a marinade for your pork. Place a lid on this bowl, with your pork, and allow the meat to marinade for 1.5 hours.
- Get a frying pan hot with oil. Stir fry, with high heat, your pork, until golden brown on all sides and fully cooked.
- Throw away marinade.

- Enjoy with rice.

Servings: 4 servings

Timing Information:

Preparation	Cooking	Total Time
10 mins	10 mins	1 hr 20 mins

Nutritional Information:

Calories	289 kcal
Carbohydrates	3.6 g
Cholesterol	55 mg
Fat	20.1 g
Fiber	0.1 g
Protein	18.8 g
Sodium	491 mg

* Percent Daily Values are based on a 2,000 calorie diet.

SAUCE FOR SHRIMP

(エビの醤油)

Ingredients

- 2 cups mayonnaise
- 1/2 cup water
- 1 tsp white sugar
- 1 tsp paprika
- 1 tsp garlic juice
- 1 tbsp ketchup
- 1 tsp ground ginger
- 1 tsp hot pepper sauce
- 1 tsp ground mustard
- 1/4 tsp salt
- 3/4 tsp ground white pepper

Directions

- Get a bowl and combine all the ingredients.
- Serve at room temperature. But store chilled.
- Enjoy.

Servings: 2 1/2 cups

Timing Information:

Preparation	Cooking	Total Time
5 mins		5 mins

Nutritional Information:

Calories	161 kcal
Carbohydrates	1.3 g
Cholesterol	8 mg
Fat	17.5 g
Fiber	0.1 g
Protein	0.3 g
Sodium	172 mg

* Percent Daily Values are based on a 2,000 calorie diet.

ONION SOUP

(オニオンスープ)

Ingredients

- 1/2 stalk celery, diced
- 1 small onion, diced
- 1/2 carrot, diced
- 1 tsp grated fresh ginger root
- 1/4 tsp minced fresh garlic
- 2 tbsps chicken stock
- 3 tsps beef bouillon granules
- 1 cup chopped fresh shiitake mushrooms
- 2 quarts water
- 1 cup baby Portobello mushrooms, sliced
- 1 tbsp minced fresh chives

Directions

- Get a saucepan with high heat. Get the following items boiling before continuing: water, celery, beef bouillon, onion, chicken

stock, carrots, half of the mushrooms, ginger, and garlic.
- Put a lid on the boiling contents. Set heat to a medium level. Let the contents lightly boil for 45 mins.
- Get another saucepan. Put the other half of mushrooms in it. Once the first pot has been cooking for 45 mins. Strain soup into the pot with uncooked mushrooms.
- Throw away anything left from the straining.
- Garnish with chives when served.
- Enjoy.

Servings: 6 servings

Timing Information:

Preparation	Cooking	Total Time
15 mins	45 mins	1 hr

Nutritional Information:

Calories	25 kcal
Carbohydrates	4.4 g
Cholesterol	1 mg
Fat	0.2 g
Fiber	0.9 g
Protein	1.4 g
Sodium	257 mg

* Percent Daily Values are based on a 2,000 calorie diet.

BEEF ROLLS JAPANESE STYLE

(牛肉ロール)

Ingredients

- 1 tbsp vegetable oil
- 12 shiitake mushrooms, sliced
- 24 spears fresh asparagus, trimmed
- 8 thin-cut top round steaks
- 1/4 cup soy sauce
- 1 bunch green onions, green parts only

Directions

- Get a frying pan hot with oil. Place mushrooms in the pan. Put a lid on the pan. Set the heat to low. Cook until the mushrooms are soft, but not browned.
- Boil some water in a second pot and fill a bowl with ice and water. Once the water is boiling. Dip your asparagus in the boiling water and then enter the asparagus into the ice water. Put

to the side. (Do this for all spears.)

- Heat your broiler. Apply some oil or nonstick spray to a broiler pan.
- Flatten steaks to 1/4 of an inch. Coat them with soy sauce then layer the following: 3 asparagus pieces, some mushrooms, and some green onions.
- Shape the steak into a roll-up. The seam portion of the steak should be placed at the bottom. Put a toothpick through each roll.
- Broil the steak for 4 mins. Then turn them. Broil for 3 mins.
- Be careful not to burn them.
- Enjoy.

Servings: 8 servings

Timing Information:

Preparation	Cooking	Total Time
30 mins	10 mins	40 mins

Nutritional Information:

Calories	689 kcal
Carbohydrates	5.9 g
Cholesterol	242 mg
Fat	29.1 g
Fiber	2.1 g
Protein	95.1 g
Sodium	583 mg

* Percent Daily Values are based on a 2,000 calorie diet.

CROQUETTES

(コロッケ)

Ingredients

- 3 medium russet potatoes, peeled, and chopped
- 1 tbsp butter
- 1 tbsp vegetable oil
- 3 onions, diced
- 3/4 pound ground beef
- 4 tsps light soy sauce
- all-purpose flour for coating
- 2 eggs, beaten
- panko bread crumbs
- 1/2 cup oil for frying

Directions

- Get a saucepan. Boil salted water and potatoes for 16 mins. Remove water and put potatoes in a separate bowl. Combine some butter with the potatoes and mash them.
- Get a frying pan. Heat 1 tbsp of oil. Stir fry onions until soft. Add

your soy sauce and beef to the onions.

- Continue to stir fry beef until browned and no liquid remains.
- Mix beef with the potatoes evenly.
- Get another frying pan hot with half a cup of oil.
- Form your mashed potatoes and beef into 10 patties and coat them with flour, then eggs, then bread crumbs.
- Finally fry each patty until golden on all sides.
- Remove excess oil and enjoy.

Servings: 10 servings

Timing Information:

Preparation	Cooking	Total Time
10 mins	20 mins	30 mins

Nutritional Information:

Calories	239 kcal
Carbohydrates	20.4 g
Cholesterol	69 mg
Fat	3.9 g
Fiber	1.5 g
Protein	9.6 g
Sodium	196 mg

* Percent Daily Values are based on a 2,000 calorie diet.

CABBAGE JAPANESE INSPIRED

(キャベツ)

Ingredients

- 3 tbsps sesame oil
- 3 tbsps rice vinegar
- 1 clove garlic, minced (optional)
- 1 tsp grated fresh ginger root (optional)
- 1 tbsp white sugar (optional)
- 1 tsp salt
- 1 tsp black pepper
- 1/2 large head cabbage, cored and shredded
- 1 bunch green onions, thinly sliced
- 1 cup almond slivers
- 1/4 cup toasted sesame seeds

Directions

- Combine all the ingredients in a large bowl. Mix the wet ingredient first, then the dry

ones. Toss everything so the cabbage is evenly coated.
- Enjoy at room temperature or chilled.

Servings: 12 servings

Timing Information:

Preparation	Cooking	Total Time
25 mins		25 mins

Nutritional Information:

Calories	126 kcal
Carbohydrates	8.1 g
Cholesterol	0 mg
Fat	9.6 g
Fiber	3 g
Protein	3.5 g
Sodium	208 mg

* Percent Daily Values are based on a 2,000 calorie diet.

FRIED SHRIMP IN JAPAN

(フライドチキン)

Ingredients

- 1 pound medium shrimp, peeled (tails left on) and deveined
- 1/2 tsp salt
- 1/2 tsp ground black pepper
- 1/2 tsp garlic powder
- 1 cup all-purpose flour
- 1 tsp paprika
- 2 eggs, beaten
- 1 cup panko crumbs
- 1 quart vegetable oil for frying

Directions

- Get 4 bowls: Bowl 1. Should have shrimp with garlic powder, pepper and salt. Bowl 2. Should have paprika and flour. Bowl 3 should have bread crumbs. Bowl 4 should have whisked eggs.
- Get a frying pan or deep fryer. Get it hot for frying about 375

degrees. Coat shrimp with flour, then with egg, and then with bread crumbs.

- Deep fry your shrimp in batches for 4 to 7 mins. Remove excess oil with paper towel.
- Enjoy with shrimp sauce.

Servings: 1 pound

Timing Information:

Preparation	Cooking	Total Time
10 mins	10 mins	20 mins

Nutritional Information:

Calories	630 kcal
Carbohydrates	53.7 g
Cholesterol	250 mg
Fat	36.6 g
Fiber	1.5 g
Protein	28.3 g
Sodium	763 mg

* Percent Daily Values are based on a 2,000 calorie diet.

FRIED CHICKEN FROM JAPAN

(フライドチキン)

Ingredients

- 2 eggs, lightly beaten
- 1/2 tsp salt
- 1/2 tsp black pepper
- 1/2 tsp white sugar
- 1 tbsp minced garlic
- 1 tbsp grated fresh ginger root
- 1 tbsp sesame oil
- 1 tbsp soy sauce
- 1/8 tsp chicken bouillon granules
- 1 1/2 pounds skinless, boneless chicken breast halves - cut into 1 inch cubes
- 3 tbsps potato starch
- 1 tbsp rice flour
- oil for frying

Directions

- Get a bowl and combine the following: bouillon, eggs, soy sauce, salt, sesame oil, pepper, ginger, garlic, and sugar. Use as a marinade for the chicken. Place a lid over the contents. And let the chicken marinate in this mixture at least 35 mins in the frig.

- Take off the lid from the marinade and add rice flour and potato starch to it. Evenly combine everything.
- Get a frying pan and get oil to 365 degrees.
- Fry your chicken until brown in a batch process.
- Remove excess oil.
- Enjoy.

Servings: 8 servings

Timing Information:

Preparation	Cooking	Total Time
20 mins	20 mins	1 hr 10 mins

Nutritional Information:

Calories	256 kcal
Carbohydrates	4.8 g
Cholesterol	98 mg
Fat	16.7 g
Fiber	0.1 g
Protein	20.9 g
Sodium	327 mg

* Percent Daily Values are based on a 2,000 calorie diet.

Katsu

Ingredients

- 4 skinless, boneless chicken breast halves - pounded to 1/2 inch thickness
- salt and pepper to taste
- 2 tbsps all-purpose flour
- 1 egg, beaten
- 1 cup panko bread crumbs
- 1 cup oil for frying, or as needed

Directions

- Get three bowls. Bowl 1 for chicken with some pepper and salt. Bowl 2 for bread crumbs. Bowl 3 for eggs.
- Cover chicken with flour first. Then with egg, and finally with crumbs.
- Get a frying pan and heat 1/4 inch of oil. Fry your chicken for 5 mins on each side.
- Remove excess oil.
- Enjoy.

Servings: 4 servings

Timing Information:

Preparation	Cooking	Total Time
10 mins	10 mins	20 mins

Nutritional Information:

Calories	297 kcal
Carbohydrates	22.2 g
Cholesterol	118 mg
Fat	11.4 g
Fiber	0.1 g
Protein	31.2 g
Sodium	251 mg

* Percent Daily Values are based on a 2,000 calorie diet.

JAPANESE SPINACH

(ほうれん草)

Ingredients

- 2 tbsps sesame oil
- 1 tbsp brown sugar
- 10 cups fresh spinach leaves
- 4 tbsps black sesame seeds, toasted

Directions

- Get a frying pan and get sesame oil hot. Combine spinach with oil in 3 cup batches. Fry until completely wilted. Then mix in another 3 cups of spinach.
- Smash your sesame seeds into small crumbs. Set to the side.
- Once your spinach is completely wilted create a hole in the center of the spinach. In the hole add sugar and cook until melted down. Mix spinach and sugar together completely.

- Serve with a garnish of crushed sesame seeds.
- Enjoy.

Servings: 6 servings

Timing Information:

Preparation	Cooking	Total Time
5 mins	2 mins	7 mins

Nutritional Information:

Calories	101 kcal
Carbohydrates	6.7 g
Cholesterol	0 mg
Fat	7.9 g
Fiber	2.5 g
Protein	3.4 g
Sodium	66 mg

* Percent Daily Values are based on a 2,000 calorie diet.

TOFU AND MISO

(豆腐みそ)

Ingredients

- 2 tbsps sesame seeds
- 1/2 cup dried Asian-style whole sardines
- 2 1/2 tbsps red miso paste
- 1/2 cup boiling water
- 1 (16 ounce) package silken tofu, cubed
- 4 green onions, thinly sliced
- crushed red pepper flakes

Directions

- Get a skillet and fry sesame seeds until aromatic for 3 mins.
- Get a pan and begin to boil water.
- Get a food processor and combine dried sardines and sesame seeds. Process into a powder.
- Put sesame and sardines in a bowl and combine miso. Combine in your boiling water (1/2 cup)

from earlier and mix until creamy.

- Finally combine your tofu red pepper, and green onions.
- Enjoy.

Servings: 6 servings

Timing Information:

Preparation	Cooking	Total Time
15 mins	2 mins	17 mins

Nutritional Information:

Calories	82 kcal
Carbohydrates	4.6 g
Cholesterol	6 mg
Fat	4.5 g
Fiber	0.9 g
Protein	7.4 g
Sodium	358 mg

* Percent Daily Values are based on a 2,000 calorie diet.

Chapter 3: Thailand

Classical Pad Thai Noodles
I

Ingredients

- 2/3 cup dried rice vermicelli
- 1/4 cup peanut oil
- 2/3 cup thinly sliced firm tofu
- 1 large egg, beaten
- 4 cloves garlic, finely chopped
- 1/4 cup vegetable broth
- 2 tbsps fresh lime juice
- 2 tbsps soy sauce
- 1 tbsp white sugar
- 1 tsp salt
- 1/2 tsp dried red chili flakes
- 3 tbsps chopped peanuts
- 1 pound bean sprouts, divided
- 3 green onions, whites cut thinly across and greens sliced into thin lengths - divided

- 3 tbsps chopped peanuts
- 2 limes, cut into wedges for garnish

Directions

- Put rice vermicelli noodles in hot water for about 30 minutes before draining the water.
- Cook tofu in hot oil until golden brown before draining it with paper tower.
- Reserve 1 tbsp of oil for later use and cook egg in the remaining hot oil until done, and set them aside for later use.
- Now cook noodles and garlic in the hot reserved oil, while coating them well with this oil along the way.
- In this pan containing noodles; add tofu, salt, chili flakes, egg and 3 tbsps peanuts, and mix all this very thoroughly.

- Also add bean sprouts and green onion into it, while reserving some for the garnishing purposes.
- Cook all this for two minutes before transferring to a serving platter.
- Garnish this with peanuts and the reserved vegetables before placing some lime wedges around the platter to make this dish more attractive.
- Serve.

Serving: 4

Timing Information:

Preparation	Cooking	Total Time
30 mins	20 mins	2 hrs

Nutritional Information:

Calories	397 kcal
Carbohydrates	39.5 g
Cholesterol	41 mg
Fat	23.3 g
Fiber	5 g
Protein	13.2 g
Sodium	1234 mg

* Percent Daily Values are based on a 2,000 calorie diet.

A Pesto From Thailand

Ingredients

- 1 bunch cilantro
- 1/4 cup peanut butter
- 3 cloves garlic, minced
- 3 tbsps extra-virgin olive oil
- 2 tbsps minced fresh ginger
- 1 1/2 tbsps fish sauce
- 1 tbsp brown sugar
- 1/2 tsp cayenne pepper

Directions

- Put all the ingredients that are mentioned above in a blender and blend it until you see that the required smoothness is achieved.

Serving: 12

Timing Information:

Preparation	Cooking	Total Time
10 mins		10 mins

Nutritional Information:

Calories	84 kcal
Carbohydrates	3.4 g
Cholesterol	0 mg
Fat	7.4 g
Fiber	0.6 g
Protein	1.9 g
Sodium	197 mg

* Percent Daily Values are based on a 2,000 calorie diet.

Easy Hummus Thai Style

Ingredients

- 1/4 cup coconut oil
- 2 large cloves garlic, very thinly sliced
- 2 cups cooked garbanzo beans
- 1/4 cup fresh lime juice
- 1/4 cup peanut butter
- 1/4 cup coconut milk
- 1/4 cup sweet chili sauce
- 1/4 cup minced lemon grass
- 1/4 cup minced fresh Thai basil leaves
- 1 tbsp grated fresh ginger
- 2 tsps green curry paste
- 1 jalapeno pepper, minced
- 1/2 tsp salt
- 1 pinch cayenne pepper(optional)
- 1 pinch chili powder (optional)

Directions

- Cook garlic in hot coconut oil for about one minute and transfer it to a bowl.
- Put cooled garlic mixture, lime juice, coconut milk, chili sauce, lemon grass, basil, ginger, curry paste, garbanzo beans, jalapeno pepper, salt, peanut butter, cayenne pepper and chili in a blender and blend it until you find that it is smooth.
- Serve.

Serving: 12

Timing Information:

Preparation	Cooking	Total Time
15 mins	5 mins	30 mins

Nutritional Information:

Calories	142 kcal
Carbohydrates	13.8 g
Cholesterol	0 mg
Fat	9.4 g
Fiber	2.4 g
Protein	3.9 g
Sodium	315 mg

* Percent Daily Values are based on a 2,000 calorie diet.

CLASSICAL PAD THAI NOODLES II

Ingredients

- 1 (6.75 ounce) package thin rice noodles
- 2 tbsps vegetable oil
- 3 ounces fried tofu, sliced into thin strips
- 1 clove garlic, minced
- 1 egg
- 1 tbsp soy sauce
- 1 pinch white sugar
- 2 tbsps chopped peanuts
- 1 cup fresh bean sprouts
- 1 tbsp chopped fresh cilantro
- 1 lime, cut into wedges

Directions

- In a heatproof bowl containing noodles, pour boiling water and let it stand as it is for about five minutes before draining the water and setting it aside for later use.

- Fry garlic in hot oil until brown before adding noodles frying it for about one minute.
- Now add egg into it and break it up when it starts to get solid, and mix it well into the noodles.
- Now add soy sauce, tofu, cilantro, bean sprouts, sugar and peanuts into it and mix it well.
- Remove from heat and add lime wedges just before you serve.

Serving: 4

Timing Information:

Preparation	Cooking	Total Time
15 mins	10 mins	25 mins

Nutritional Information:

Calories	352 kcal
Carbohydrates	46.8 g
Cholesterol	46 mg
Fat	15 g
Fiber	3 g
Protein	9.2 g
Sodium	335 mg

* Percent Daily Values are based on a 2,000 calorie diet.

SUPER EASY COCONUT SOUP THAI-STYLE

Ingredients

- 1 pound medium shrimp - peeled and deveined
- 2 (13.5 ounce) cans canned coconut milk
- 2 cups water
- 1 (1 inch) piece galangal, thinly sliced
- 4 stalks lemon grass, bruised and chopped
- 10 kaffir lime leaves, torn in half
- 1 pound shiitake mushrooms, sliced
- 1/4 cup lime juice
- 3 tbsps fish sauce
- 1/4 cup brown sugar
- 1 tsp curry powder
- 1 tbsp green onion, thinly sliced
- 1 tsp dried red pepper flakes

Directions

- Cook shrimp in boiling water until tender.
- Put coconut milk, water, lime leaves, galangal and lemon grass in a large sized pan and heat it up for about 10 minutes before transferring the coconut milk into a new pan, while discarding all the spices.
- Heat up shiitake mushrooms in the coconut milk for five minutes before adding lime juice, curry powder, brown sugar and fish sauce into it.
- When you want to serve it, heat up the shrimp in this soup for some time before pouring this into serving bowls.

Serving: 8

Timing Information:

Preparation	Cooking	Total Time
15 mins	25 mins	40 mins

Nutritional Information:

Calories	314 kcal
Carbohydrates	17.2 g
Cholesterol	86 mg
Fat	21.6 g
Fiber	2.1 g
Protein	15.3 g
Sodium	523 mg

* Percent Daily Values are based on a 2,000 calorie diet.

CURRY THAI INSPIRED CHICKEN WITH PINEAPPLE

Ingredients

- 2 cups uncooked jasmine rice
- 1 quart water
- 1/4 cup red curry paste
- 2 (13.5 ounce) cans coconut milk
- 2 skinless, boneless chicken breast halves - cut into thin strips
- 3 tbsps fish sauce
- 1/4 cup white sugar
- 1 1/2 cups sliced bamboo shoots, drained
- 1/2 red bell pepper, julienned
- 1/2 green bell pepper, julienned
- 1/2 small onion, chopped
- 1 cup pineapple chunks, drained

Directions

- Bring the mixture of rice and water to boil before turning the heat down to low and cooking for 25 minutes.

- Add coconut milk, bamboo shoots, chicken, sugar and fish sauce to the mixture of curry paste and 1 can coconut milk in a pan before bringing all this to boil and cooking for 15 minutes.
- Into this mixture, add red bell pepper, onion and green bell pepper, and cook all this for ten more minutes or until you see that the peppers are tender.
- Add pineapple after removing from heat and serve this on top of cooked rice.

Serving: 6

Timing Information:

Preparation	Cooking	Total Time
15 mins	35 mins	50 mins

Nutritional Information:

Calories	623 kcal
Carbohydrates	77.5 g
Cholesterol	20 mg
Fat	34.5 g
Fiber	3.5 g
Protein	20.3 g
Sodium	781 mg

* Percent Daily Values are based on a 2,000 calorie diet.

SIMPLE AND EASY CLASSICAL PEANUT SAUCE

Ingredients

- 1/4 cup creamy peanut butter
- 3 cloves garlic, minced
- 1/4 cup brown sugar
- 1/4 cup mayonnaise
- 1/4 cup soy sauce
- 2 tbsps fresh lemon juice

Directions

- Whisk all the ingredients that are mentioned above in a medium sized bowl and refrigerate it for at least two hours before you serve it to anyone.

Serving: 6

Timing Information:

Preparation	Cooking	Total Time
10 mins		10 mins

Nutritional Information:

Calories	130 kcal
Carbohydrates	9.8 g
Cholesterol	3 mg
Fat	9.5 g
Fiber	0.6 g
Protein	2.7 g
Sodium	529 mg

* Percent Daily Values are based on a 2,000 calorie diet.

VEGETABLE SOUP IN THAILAND

Ingredients

- 1 cup uncooked brown rice
- 2 cups water
- 3 tbsps olive oil
- 1 sweet onion, chopped
- 4 cloves garlic, minced
- 1/4 cup chopped fresh ginger root
- 1 cup chopped carrots
- 4 cups chopped broccoli
- 1 red bell pepper, diced
- 1 (14 ounce) can light coconut milk
- 6 cups vegetable broth
- 1 cup white wine
- 3 tbsps fish sauce
- 2 tbsps soy sauce
- 3 Thai chili peppers
- 2 tbsps chopped fresh lemon grass
- 1 tbsp Thai pepper garlic sauce
- 1 tsp saffron
- 3/4 cup plain yogurt

- fresh cilantro, for garnish

Directions

- Bring the mixture of rice and water to boil before turning the heat down to low and cooking for 45 minutes.
- Cook ginger, carrots, garlic and onion in hot olive oil for about five minutes before you add broccoli, coconut milk, broth, wine, soy sauce, Thai chili peppers, red bell pepper, lemon grass, fish sauce, garlic sauce, and saffron into it and cook for another 25 minutes.
- Now blend this soup in batches in a blender until you get the required smoothness.
- Mix yoghurt and cooked rice very thoroughly with this soup.
- Garnish with cilantro before you serve.

Serving: 12

Timing Information:

Preparation	Cooking	Total Time
15 mins	1 hr 15 mins	1 hr 30 mins

Nutritional Information:

Calories	183 kcal
Carbohydrates	21.4 g
Cholesterol	< 1 mg
Fat	7.4 g
Fiber	3 g
Protein	4.4 g
Sodium	749 mg

* Percent Daily Values are based on a 2,000 calorie diet.

THE BEST ORANGE THAI CHICKEN

Ingredients

- 2 tbsps olive oil
- 3 carrots, cut into matchsticks
- 1/2 tsp minced fresh ginger root
- 1 clove garlic, minced
- 2 tbsps olive oil
- 2 skinless, boneless chicken breast halves, cut into small pieces
- 1/2 cup water
- 1/2 cup peanuts
- 1/3 cup orange juice
- 1/3 cup soy sauce
- 1/3 cup brown sugar
- 2 tbsps ketchup
- 1 tsp crushed red pepper flakes
- 2 tbsps cornstarch

Directions

- Cook carrots, garlic and ginger in hot olive oil for about 5 minutes before transferring it to a bowl.
- Cook chicken in hot olive oil for about 10 minutes before adding carrot mixture, water, brown sugar , orange juice, soy sauce, peanuts, ketchup, and red pepper flakes into this, and cooking for another 5 minutes.
- Take out ¼ cup of sauce from the pan and add cornstarch into it.
- Add this cornstarch mixture back to the chicken and cook until you see that the required thickness has been reached.

Serving: 12

Timing Information:

Preparation	Cooking	Total Time
15 mins	25 mins	40 mins

Nutritional Information:

Calories	427 kcal
Carbohydrates	37.1 g
Cholesterol	32 mg
Fat	24.3 g
Fiber	3.5 g
Protein	18.4 g
Sodium	1360 mg

* Percent Daily Values are based on a 2,000 calorie diet.

Thai Broccoli Mix

Ingredients

- 2 tbsps olive oil
- 2 large skinless, boneless chicken breast halves, cut into bite-size pieces
- 1 (12 ounce) package broccoli coleslaw mix
- 1 tsp sesame oil, or to taste
- 1/2 cup water
- 1/2 cup peanut sauce (such as House of Tsang®), or to taste
- 1 pinch salt to taste

Directions

- Cook chicken in hot olive oil for about 5 minutes before you add water, broccoli and sesame oil.
- Cook this on medium heat for about 15 minutes or until you see that the broccoli slaw is tender.

- Do add some peanut sauce and salt according to your taste before serving.

Serving: 4

Timing Information:

Preparation	Cooking	Total Time
10 mins	20 mins	30 mins

Nutritional Information:

Calories	315 kcal
Carbohydrates	8.2 g
Cholesterol	65 mg
Fat	18.9 g
Fiber	3.2 g
Protein	28.3 g
Sodium	275 mg

* Percent Daily Values are based on a 2,000 calorie diet.

A UNIQUELY SIMPLE CUMBER SOUP WITH THAI ROOTS

Ingredients

- 1 tbsp vegetable oil
- 3 cucumbers, peeled and diced
- 1/2 cup chopped green onion
- 2 1/2 cups chicken broth
- 1 1/2 tbsps lemon juice
- 1 tsp white sugar
- salt and ground black pepper to taste

Directions

- Cook cucumber in hot olive oil for about 5 minutes before adding green onions and cooking for another five minutes.
- Add chicken broth, sugar and lemon juice into it before bringing all this to boil.
- Turn down the heat to low and cook for another 20 minutes

before adding salt and black
pepper according to your taste.

- Serve.

Serving: 4

Timing Information:

Preparation	Cooking	Total Time
15 mins	30 mins	45 mins

Nutritional Information:

Calories	67 kcal
Carbohydrates	6.8 g
Cholesterol	3 mg
Fat	4 g
Fiber	1.4 g
Protein	1.7 g
Sodium	702 mg

* Percent Daily Values are based on a 2,000 calorie diet.

BBQ Chicken Thai Style

Ingredients

- 1 bunch fresh cilantro with roots
- 3 cloves garlic, peeled
- 3 small red hot chili peppers, seeded and chopped
- 1 tsp ground turmeric
- 1 tsp curry powder
- 1 tbsp white sugar
- 1 pinch salt
- 3 tbsps fish sauce
- 1 (3 pound) chicken, cut into pieces
- 1/4 cup coconut milk

Directions

- At first you need to set a grill or grilling plate to medium heat and put some oil before starting anything else.
- Put minced cilantro roots, salt, leaves, chili peppers, curry

powder, turmeric, sugar, fish sauce, garlic in a blender and blend until you see that the required smoothness is achieved.

- Combine this paste and chicken in large bowl, and refrigerate it for at least three hours for margination.

- Cook this on the preheated grill for about 15 minutes each side or until tender, while brushing it regularly with coconut milk.

- Serve.

NOTE: Adjust grilling times accordingly if using a grilling plate instead of a conventional grill.

Serving: 4

Timing Information:

Preparation	Cooking	Total Time
15 mins	30 mins	4 hr 45 mins

Nutritional Information:

Calories	564 kcal
Carbohydrates	52.4 g
Cholesterol	230 mg
Fat	19.3 g
Fiber	4.3 g
Protein	46.3 g
Sodium	375 mg

* Percent Daily Values are based on a 2,000 calorie diet.

CHARONG'S FAVORITE THAI SOUP OF GINGER

Ingredients

- 3 cups coconut milk
- 2 cups water
- 1/2 pound skinless, boneless chicken breast halves - cut into thin strips
- 3 tbsps minced fresh ginger root
- 2 tbsps fish sauce, or to taste
- 1/4 cup fresh lime juice
- 2 tbsps sliced green onions
- 1 tbsp chopped fresh cilantro

Directions

- Bring the mixture of coconut milk and water to boil before adding chicken strips, and cooking it for three minutes on medium heat or until you see that the chicken is cooked through.

- Now add ginger, green onions, lime juice, cilantro and fish sauce into it.
- Mix it well and serve.

Serving: 4

Timing Information:

Preparation	Cooking	Total Time
15 mins	10 mins	25 mins

Nutritional Information:

Calories	415 kcal
Carbohydrates	7.3 g
Cholesterol	29 mg
Fat	39 g
Fiber	2.1 g
Protein	14.4 g
Sodium	598 mg

* Percent Daily Values are based on a 2,000 calorie diet.

Chicken Curry I

Ingredients

- 1 tbsp olive oil
- 3 tbsps Thai yellow curry paste (such as Mae Ploy®)
- 1 pound cooked skinless, boneless chicken breast, cut into bite-size pieces
- 2 (14 ounce) cans coconut milk
- 1 cup chicken stock
- 1 yellow onion, chopped
- 3 small red potatoes, cut into cubes, or as needed
- 3 red Thai chili peppers, chopped with seeds, or more to taste
- 1 tsp fish sauce

Directions

- Mix curry paste in hot oil before adding chicken and coating it well.

- Add 1 can coconut milk and cook it for five minutes before adding the rest of the coconut milk, onion, potatoes, chicken stock and chili peppers into it and bringing all this to boil.
- Turn the heat down to low and cook for 25 minutes or until the potatoes are tender.
- Add fish sauce into before serving.
- Enjoy.

Serving: 6

Timing Information:

Preparation	Cooking	Total Time
15 mins	40 mins	55 mins

Nutritional Information:

Calories	500 kcal
Carbohydrates	22.1 g
Cholesterol	58 mg
Fat	36.1 g
Fiber	3.6 g
Protein	25.8 g
Sodium	437 mg

* Percent Daily Values are based on a 2,000 calorie diet.

Chicken Curry II

Ingredients

- 1 tbsp canola oil
- 2 tbsps green curry paste
- 1 pound boneless skinless chicken breasts, cut into bite-size pieces
- 1 small onion, thinly sliced
- 1 red pepper, cut into thin strips, then cut crosswise in half
- 1 green pepper, cut into thin strips, then cut crosswise in half
- 4 ounces cream cheese, cubed
- 1/4 cup milk
- 1/8 tsp white pepper
- 2 cups hot cooked long-grain white rice

Directions

- Combine curry paste and hot oil before adding chicken and onions.

- Cook this for about 8 minutes before adding green and red peppers, and cooking for another five minutes.
- Now add cream cheese, white pepper and milk, and cook until you see that the cheese has melted.
- Serve this on top of rice.
- Enjoy.

Serving: 4

Timing Information:

Preparation	Cooking	Total Time
15 mins		35 mins

Nutritional Information:

Calories	621 kcal
Carbohydrates	86.7 g
Cholesterol	91 mg
Fat	19.4 g
Fiber	2.1 g
Protein	35.2 g
Sodium	316 mg

* Percent Daily Values are based on a 2,000 calorie diet.

A Thai Soup of Veggies

Ingredients

- 1/4 cup butter
- 6 tomatoes, peeled and quartered
- 3 zucchini, cut into chunks
- 1 yellow onion, cut in half and quartered
- 1 red bell pepper, chopped
- 3 cloves garlic, roughly chopped
- 1/4 cup chopped fresh cilantro leaves
- 1 tbsp chopped fresh basil (preferably Thai basil)
- 1 tbsp lime juice
- 1 pinch salt
- 2 1/2 cups milk
- 3 tbsps coconut butter
- 1 tbsp curry powder
- 1/4 tsp ground turmeric
- 1/4 tsp ground ginger
- 1/8 tsp ground cumin
- 1 bay leaf

- 5 tbsps heavy whipping cream (optional)

Directions

- Cook tomatoes, zucchini, onion, garlic, cilantro, red bell pepper, basil, lime juice, and salt in hot butter for about 25 minutes before transferring it to a blender and blending it until the required smoothness is achieved.
- Cook milk, curry powder, turmeric, ginger, coconut butter, cumin, and bay leaf in the same pan for about 5 minutes or until you see that coconut butter has melted.
- At the very end, add blended vegetables into it and cook for five more minutes.
- Garnish with heavy cream before serving.

Serving: 5

Timing Information:

Preparation	Cooking	Total Time
15 mins	35 mins	50 mins

Nutritional Information:

Calories	310 kcal
Carbohydrates	22.9 g
Cholesterol	55 mg
Fat	22.4 g
Fiber	5.7 g
Protein	8.5 g
Sodium	147 mg

* Percent Daily Values are based on a 2,000 calorie diet.

CHICKEN BURGERS RE-IMAGINED FROM THAILAND

Ingredients

- 1 cup mayonnaise
- 1/4 cup flaked coconut, finely chopped
- 1 tbsp chopped fresh mint
- 2 pounds ground chicken
- 2 1/2 cups panko bread crumbs
- 1/2 cup Thai peanut sauce
- 2 tbsps red curry paste
- 2 tbsps minced green onion
- 2 tbsps minced fresh parsley
- 2 tsps soy sauce
- 3 cloves garlic, minced
- 2 tsps lemon juice
- 2 tsps lime juice
- 1 tbsp hot pepper sauce
- 8 hamburger buns, split and toasted

Directions

- At first you need to set a grill or grilling plate to medium heat and put some oil before starting anything else.
- Refrigerate a mixture of mayonnaise, mint and coconut for one hour.
- Combine ground chicken, Thai peanut sauce, curry paste, parsley, soy sauce, garlic, lemon juice, green onion, panko crumbs, lime juice, and hot pepper sauce in large sized bowl.
- Cook this on the preheated grill for about 8 minutes each side or until tender.
- Serve this with toasted bun.

NOTE: Adjust grilling times accordingly if using a grilling plate instead of a conventional grill.

Serving: 8

Timing Information:

Preparation	Cooking	Total Time
15 mins	15 mins	30 mins

Nutritional Information:

Calories	612 kcal
Carbohydrates	50.9 g
Cholesterol	80 mg
Fat	35.4 g
Fiber	2 g
Protein	36.5 g
Sodium	859 mg

* Percent Daily Values are based on a 2,000 calorie diet.

CLASSICAL SHRIMP IN THAILAND

Ingredients

- 4 cloves garlic, peeled
- 1 (1 inch) piece fresh ginger root
- 1 fresh jalapeno pepper, seeded
- 1/2 tsp salt
- 1/2 tsp ground turmeric
- 2 tbsps vegetable oil
- 1 medium onion, diced
- 1 pound medium shrimp - peeled and deveined
- 2 tomatoes, seeded and diced
- 1 cup coconut milk
- 3 tbsps chopped fresh basil leaves

Directions

- Blend the mixture of garlic, turmeric, ginger and jalapeno in a blender until the required smoothness is achieved.

- Cook onion in hot oil for a few minutes before adding spice paste and cooking for another few minutes.
- Cook shrimp for a few minutes in it before adding tomatoes and coconut milk, and cooking it for five minutes covered with lid.
- Now cook for five more minutes without lid to get the sauce thick.
- Also add some fresh basil at the last minute.
- Serve.

Serving: 4

Timing Information:

Preparation	Cooking	Total Time
10 mins	20 mins	30 mins

Nutritional Information:

Calories	289 kcal
Carbohydrates	8.2 g
Cholesterol	173 mg
Fat	20.1 g
Fiber	2.1 g
Protein	20.9 g
Sodium	502 mg

* Percent Daily Values are based on a 2,000 calorie diet.

DELIGHTFULLY THAI BASIL CHICKEN

Ingredients

- 2 tbsps peanut oil
- 1/4 cup minced garlic
- 1 pound ground chicken breast
- 12 Thai chilis, sliced into thin rings
- 2 tsps black soy sauce
- 2 tbsps fish sauce
- 1 cup fresh basil leaves

Directions

- Cook garlic in hot peanut oil for about twenty seconds before adding ground chicken and cooking for another two minutes or until the chicken loses any pinkness.
- Now add sliced chilies, fish sauce and soy sauce into it before

cooking for 15 seconds to get the chilies tender.
- At the very end, add basil and cook until you see that basil has wilted.
- Serve.

Serving: 4

Timing Information:

Preparation	Cooking	Total Time
15 mins	5 mins	20 mins

Nutritional Information:

Calories	273 kcal
Carbohydrates	16.5 g
Cholesterol	69 mg
Fat	10.7 g
Fiber	2.4 g
Protein	29.4 g
Sodium	769 mg

* Percent Daily Values are based on a 2,000 calorie diet.

A PIZZA FROM THAILAND

Ingredients

- 1 (12 inch) pre-baked pizza crust
- 1 (7 ounce) jar peanut sauce
- 1/4 cup peanut butter
- 8 ounces cooked skinless, boneless chicken breast halves, cut into strips
- 1 cup shredded Italian cheese blend
- 1 bunch green onions, chopped
- 1/2 cup fresh bean sprouts(optional)
- 1/2 cup shredded carrot(optional)
- 1 tbsp chopped roasted peanuts (optional)

Directions

- Preheat your oven to 400 degrees F.
- Spread a mixture of peanut sauce and peanut butter over the pizza

crust and also put some strips of chicken, green onions and cheese.

- Bake in the preheated oven for about 12 minutes or until the cheese has melted.
- Garnish with carrot shreds, peanuts and sprouts.
- Serve.

Serving: 8

Timing Information:

Preparation	Cooking	Total Time
10 mins	10 mins	20 mins

Nutritional Information:

Calories	396 kcal
Carbohydrates	33.3 g
Cholesterol	37 mg
Fat	20.2 g
Fiber	3.3 g
Protein	24.2 g
Sodium	545 mg

* Percent Daily Values are based on a 2,000 calorie diet.

Spicy Thai Pasta

Ingredients

- 1 (12 ounce) package rice vermicelli
- 1 large tomato, diced
- 4 green onions, diced
- 2 pounds cooked shrimp, peeled and deveined
- 1 1/2 cups prepared Thai peanut sauce

Directions

- Add rice vermicelli into boiling water and cook for about five minutes or until done.
- Combine this rice with tomato, peanut sauce, green onions and shrimp very thoroughly in a medium sized bowl before refrigerating for at least eight hours.

Serving: 8

Timing Information:

Preparation	Cooking	Total Time
15 mins	5 mins	20 mins

Nutritional Information:

Calories	564 kcal
Carbohydrates	52.4 g
Cholesterol	230 mg
Fat	19.3 g
Fiber	4.3 g
Protein	46.3 g
Sodium	375 mg

* Percent Daily Values are based on a 2,000 calorie diet.

CHAPTER 4: THE PHILIPPINES

FILIPINO OXTAIL STEW

Ingredients:

- 1 1/2 pounds beef oxtail, cut into pieces
- 1 large onion, quartered
- 2 cloves garlic, chopped
- 1 tsp salt
- 1/2 tsp ground black pepper, or to taste
- 1 large eggplant, cut into 2-inch chunks
- 1/2 head bok choy, cut into 1-inch pieces
- 1/2 pound fresh green beans, trimmed and snapped into 2-inch pieces
- 1/4 cup peanut butter, or as needed to thicken sauce

Directions:

- Bring the mixture of oxtail pieces, pepper, garlic and salt to boil in water before cooking it for two hours over medium heat.
- Now add eggplant, green beans and bok choy into this mixture before cooking it for another 20 minutes or until the vegetables you just added are tender.
- Add a mixture of peanut butter and some broth into the stew just before you serve it.

Serving: 6

Timing Information:

Preparation	Cooking	Total Time
2 hr 20 mins	2 hr 20 mins	2 hr 35 mins

Nutritional Information:

Calories	395 kcal
Carbohydrates	14.9 g
Cholesterol	125 mg
Fat	21 g
Fiber	6.6 g
Protein	40.1 g
Sodium	683 mg

* Percent Daily Values are based on a 2,000 calorie diet.

BUKO I

(COCONUT CHILLER)

Ingredients

- 2 fresh young coconuts
- 1 cup water
- 1 tbsp white sugar, or to taste
- ice cubes

Directions

- Cut the top of a coconut and pour its juice into a bowl.
- Slice the coconut into two pieces and scrap out its inner flesh into the bowl containing the juice.
- Now mix sugar and some water, and pour it over ice in a glass.
- Serve.

Serving: 2

Timing Information:

Preparation	Cooking	Total Time
15 mins		15 mins

Nutritional Information:

Calories	1430 kcal
Carbohydrates	66.7 g
Cholesterol	0 mg
Fat	133 g
Fiber	35.7 g
Protein	13.2 g
Sodium	87 mg

* Percent Daily Values are based on a 2,000 calorie diet.

BIKO

(FILIPINO SWEET BAKED RICE)

Ingredients:

- 4 cups uncooked glutinous white rice
- 6 cups cold water
- 1 (14 ounce) can coconut milk, divided
- 1 1/3 cups white sugar
- 1 1/3 cups brown sugar
- 3 tbsps coconut preserves (such as Phil Supreme)

Directions:

- Preheat your oven to 325 degrees F and grease the baking pan.
- Cook rice that has been soaked in water for at least 8 hours along with half a cup of coconut milk, white sugar and water until the rice is tender.

- Now pour this mixture into the already prepared baking pan and pour a boiled mixture of coconut milk, brown sugar and coconut preserves over the rice.
- Bake in the preheated oven for about 25 minutes and cut into squares.
- Serve.

Serving: 6

Timing Information:

Preparation	Cooking	Total Time
15 mins	45 mins	11 hr

Nutritional Information:

Calories	463 kcal
Carbohydrates	90.3 g
Cholesterol	0 mg
Fat	9.5 g
Fiber	2.1 g
Protein	5.4 g
Sodium	17 mg

* Percent Daily Values are based on a 2,000 calorie diet.

TULYA

Ingredients:

- 2 tbsps olive oil
- 1 onion, chopped
- 2 cloves garlic, minced
- 1 (2 inch) piece fresh ginger, peeled and grated
- 2 tbsps oyster sauce
- 1/2 cup water
- 2 1/4 pounds clams in shell, scrubbed

Directions:

- Cook onion, garlic and ginger in hot oil for about 5 minutes before adding oyster sauce and cooking for another 2 minutes.
- Pour water into the mix and cook for another two minutes while covering the pan.
- Now add clams and cook for another 5 minutes or until the clams have opened up.

- Discard all the unopened clams and serve.

Serving: 6

Timing Information:

Preparation	Cooking	Total Time
15 mins	10 mins	25 mins

Nutritional Information:

Calories	120 kcal
Carbohydrates	5.3 g
Cholesterol	20 mg
Fat	7.4 g
Fiber	0.6 g
Protein	8.1 g
Sodium	91 mg

* Percent Daily Values are based on a 2,000 calorie diet.

SATI BABI

Ingredients:

- 3 pounds pork butt roast, cut into 1 1/2 inch cubes
- 3/4 tsp salt
- 1/8 tsp ground black pepper
- 1 tbsp ground coriander
- 1 tbsp cumin seed
- 1/2 tsp vegetable oil
- 1/2 cup sliced onions
- 1 tbsp brown sugar
- 1/3 cup soy sauce
- 1/4 tsp ground ginger
- 3 limes, cut into wedges

Directions:

- At first you need to set a grill or grilling plate to medium heat and put some oil before starting anything else.
- Combine salt, pepper, coriander, cumin seed, and vegetable oil in a

dish before adding pork and letting it stand for at least 20 minutes.

- Now add onion, ginger and soy sauce and place everything in the refrigerator for at least one hour after mixing it well.
- Thread these pork cubes onto the skewers
- Cook contents on the preheated grill or grilling plate for about 15 minutes or until tender.
- Sprinkle some lime juice before serving.
- Enjoy.

Serving: 6

Timing Information:

Preparation	Cooking	Total Time
15 mins	15 mins	1 hr 30 mins

Nutritional Information:

Calories	224 kcal
Carbohydrates	6.6 g
Cholesterol	71 mg
Fat	13 g
Fiber	1.4 g
Protein	20.2 g
Sodium	873 mg

* Percent Daily Values are based on a 2,000 calorie diet.

Barbecued Spareribs

Ingredients:

- 1 (4 pound) package pork spareribs, rinsed and patted dry
- salt and ground black pepper to taste
- 1 cup water
- 1 cup sweet chili sauce

Directions:

- Preheat your oven to 350 degrees F and grease the baking pan.
- Add some salt and pepper over spareribs before putting them into the baking dish containing water.
- Cover with aluminum foil.
- Bake in the preheated oven for about 30 minutes before pouring chili sauce half of what we have and return it to the oven.

- Brush with chili sauce every five minutes and continue baking for 30 more minutes or until tender.
- Serve.

Serving: 6

Timing Information:

Preparation	Cooking	Total Time
10 mins	1 hr	1 hr 10 mins

Nutritional Information:

Calories	710 kcal
Carbohydrates	20.6 g
Cholesterol	192 mg
Fat	48.4 g
Fiber	1.4 g
Protein	46.1 g
Sodium	765 mg

* Percent Daily Values are based on a 2,000 calorie diet.

FILIPINO MELON DESSERT I

Ingredients

- 1 large ripe cantaloupe
- 2 quarts cold water
- 1 large honeydew melon

Directions

- Blend cantaloupe and place it in a pitcher.
- Now pour into it some water and refrigerate it for 12 hours or preferably overnight.
- Make small balls out of the honeydew melon using a spoon and add these balls before serving.

Serving: 6

Timing Information:

Preparation	Cooking	Total Time
20 mins		1 day

Nutritional Information:

Calories	123 kcal
Carbohydrates	30.5 g
Cholesterol	0 mg
Fat	0.6 g
Fiber	2.8 g
Protein	2.3 g
Sodium	70 mg

* Percent Daily Values are based on a 2,000 calorie diet.

CHICKEN ADOBO

Ingredients:

- 1 1/2 cups water
- 1 cup distilled white vinegar
- 4 tbsps soy sauce
- 1 tsp whole peppercorns
- 4 cloves garlic, crushed
- 2 tbsps salt
- 1 (2 to 3 pound) whole chicken, cut into pieces
- 2 tbsps vegetable oil

Directions:

- Mix water, salt, vinegar, peppercorns, garlic and soy sauce before adding chicken and cooking it over low heat for about 30 minutes or until the chicken is tender.
- Cook this chicken in hot oil until brown after removing it from the pot.

- Now put this chicken back into the pot and cook over medium heat until you see that the liquid has become thick.
- Serve.

Serving: 6

Timing Information:

Preparation	Cooking	Total Time
1 hr	15 mins	1 hr 15 mins

Nutritional Information:

Calories	340 kcal
Carbohydrates	2 g
Cholesterol	100 mg
Fat	21.5 g
Fiber	0.2 g
Protein	32.5 g
Sodium	3598 mg

* Percent Daily Values are based on a 2,000 calorie diet.

EMPANADA PORK FILLING

Ingredients:

- 1 pound ground pork
- salt and pepper to taste
- 2 tbsps olive oil
- 1 onion, chopped
- 2 cloves garlic, minced
- 1 (9 ounce) box frozen peas and carrots
- 1 (1.5 ounce) box raisins
- 1 small potato, diced

Directions:

- Take out ground pork and cook it over medium heat in nonstick skillet for about 5 minutes or until you see that it is brown.
- Now cook onion and garlic in hot oil for about 5 minutes before adding browned pork into it and cooking it for another 5 minutes.

- Now add potato, raisins, peas and carrots into the skillet, and cook them for about 10 minutes or until the vegetables are tender.
- Allow this to cool down before filling into empanada dough.
- Serve.

Serving: 6

Timing Information:

Preparation	Cooking	Total Time
10 mins	15 mins	1 hr 25 mins

Nutritional Information:

Calories	67 kcal
Carbohydrates	4.4 g
Cholesterol	12 mg
Fat	3.9 g
Fiber	0.7 g
Protein	4 g
Sodium	19 mg

* Percent Daily Values are based on a 2,000 calorie diet.

FRIED TULINGAN (MACKEREL)

Ingredients:

- 1 (3 1/2) pound whole mackerel, gutted and cleaned
- 2 cups water
- 1 tbsp tamarind soup base
- 1 tsp fish sauce
- oil for frying

Directions:

- Mix mackerel water, fish sauce and a tamarind soup base in a skillet, and cook over medium heat for about 15 minutes.
- Flip the fish once very carefully and cook for another 15 minutes before turning off the heat and letting it stand as it is for about one hour.
- Take out the fish and dry it with paper towels before deep frying it

in large skillet for about 10 minutes.

- Serve.

Serving: 4

Timing Information:

Preparation	Cooking	Total Time
10 mins	40 mins	1 hr 50 mins

Nutritional Information:

Calories	974 kcal
Carbohydrates	0.8 g
Cholesterol	222 mg
Fat	70 g
Fiber	0 g
Protein	77.6 g
Sodium	841 mg

* Percent Daily Values are based on a 2,000 calorie diet.

Salmon Stew (Abalos Style)

Ingredients:

- 1 tbsp olive oil
- 4 cloves garlic, minced
- 1 onion, diced
- 1 tomato, diced
- 1 (14.75 ounce) can pink salmon
- 2 1/2 cups water
- bay leaf (optional)
- salt and ground black pepper to taste
- 1 tsp fish sauce (optional)

Directions:

- Cook onion and garlic in hot oil for about 5 minutes before adding tomato and salmon into it.
- Cook for another 3 minutes and then add water, fish sauce, bay leaf, salt and pepper.
- Cover the skillet and cook for 20 minutes.

- Serve.

Serving: 4

Timing Information:

Preparation	Cooking	Total Time
10 mins	15 mins	25 mins

Nutritional Information:

Calories	223 kcal
Carbohydrates	4.8 g
Cholesterol	45 mg
Fat	11 g
Fiber	0.9 g
Protein	24.9 g
Sodium	466 mg

* Percent Daily Values are based on a 2,000 calorie diet.

FILIPINO FRUIT SALAD

Ingredients

- 1 (30 ounce) can fruit cocktail, drained
- 1 (15 ounce) can lychees, drained
- 1 (12 ounce) jar macapuno (coconut preserves), drained
- 1 (20 ounce) can palm seeds, drained
- 1 (15 ounce) can creamed corn
- 1 Red Delicious apple, cored and diced
- 1 Asian pear, cored and cubed
- 1 (8 ounce) container sour cream
- 1 (14 ounce) can sweetened condensed milk

Directions

- Combine all the ingredients mentioned above in a bowl and serve it cold.

Serving: 10

Timing Information:

Preparation	Cooking	Total Time
10 mins		1 hr 10 mins

Nutritional Information:

Calories	482 kcal
Carbohydrates	61.8 g
Cholesterol	23 mg
Fat	25.9 g
Fiber	2.9 g
Protein	9.8 g
Sodium	204 mg

* Percent Daily Values are based on a 2,000 calorie diet.

FILIPINO SPAGHETTI

Ingredients:

- 2 pounds spaghetti
- 1 tbsp vegetable oil
- 1 head garlic, minced
- 1 onion, chopped
- 1 pound ground beef
- 1 pound ground pork
- salt and pepper to taste
- 1 (26.5 ounce) can spaghetti sauce
- 1 (14 ounce) jar banana ketchup
- 1/4 cup white sugar
- 1/2 cup water
- 1 pound hot dogs, sliced diagonally
- 1/2 cup shredded Cheddar cheese

Directions:

- Cook spaghetti in boiling hot salty water over high heat for about 12 minutes or until the pasta is heated through.

- Drain it well using colander.
- Now cook onion and garlic in hot oil over medium heat for about 5 minutes before adding beef and pork, while seasoning it with some salt and pepper.
- Cook it until you see the brown color on the meat and then add spaghetti sauce, water, banana ketchup and sugar into it.
- Cook until you see that the sauce has thickened before adding hot dog slices and cooking it until the hot dogs are heated through.
- Pour this over spaghetti and also some cheddar cheese.
- Enjoy.

Serving: 6

Timing Information:

Preparation	Cooking	Total Time
10 mins	10 mins	20 mins

Nutritional Information:

Calories	708 kcal
Carbohydrates	82.9 g
Cholesterol	77 mg
Fat	27.4 g
Fiber	4.3 g
Protein	29.2 g
Sodium	1085 mg

* Percent Daily Values are based on a 2,000 calorie diet.

Avocado Milkshakes in the Philippines

Ingredients

- 1 avocado - peeled, pitted, and cubed
- 5 cubes ice
- 3 tbsps white sugar
- 1 1/3 cups milk
- 1 tsp fresh lemon or lime juice
- 1 scoop vanilla ice cream

Directions

- Blend all the ingredients mentioned above in a blender until required smoothness is achieved.
- Serve.

Serving: 6

Timing Information:

Preparation	Cooking	Total Time
5 mins		5 mins

Nutritional Information:

Calories	336 kcal
Carbohydrates	37.6 g
Cholesterol	18 mg
Fat	19.1 g
Fiber	6.8 g
Protein	7.8 g
Sodium	84 mg

* Percent Daily Values are based on a 2,000 calorie diet.

Singkamas

(Jicama Salad)

Ingredients

- 1 large jicama, peeled and cut into matchsticks
- 1 red bell pepper, cut into long thin strips
- 1 green bell pepper, cut into long thin strips
- 1 small red onion, sliced into thin lengthwise slivers
- 2 green chile peppers, halved lengthwise, seeded, and cut into strips
- 1 (2 inch) piece fresh ginger root, thinly sliced
- 1 carrot, cut into matchsticks
- 1 cup water
- 2/3 cup vinegar
- 2/3 cup white sugar
- 1 tsp salt

Directions

- Mix jicama, red bell pepper, red onion, green chili peppers, ginger, green bell pepper and carrot in large sized bowl.
- In another bowl, mix water, salt, vinegar and sugar.
- Pour this mixture over the vegetables and refrigerate it for about 1 hour at least before serving it.

Serving: 10

Timing Information:

Preparation	Cooking	Total Time
30 mins		1 hr 30 mins

Nutritional Information:

Calories	113 kcal
Carbohydrates	27.5 g
Cholesterol	0 mg
Fat	0.2 g
Fiber	6.8 g
Protein	1.4 g
Sodium	244 mg

* Percent Daily Values are based on a 2,000 calorie diet.

Picadillo Filipino

(Hamburger Abalos Soup)

Ingredients

- 1 tbsp cooking oil
- 1 onion, diced
- 4 cloves garlic, minced
- 1 large tomato, diced
- 1 pound ground beef
- 4 cups water
- 1 large potato, diced
- 2 tbsps beef bouillon
- 2 tbsps fish sauce
- salt and pepper to taste

Directions

- Cook onions and garlic in hot oil over medium heat until tender add tomatoes and cook for another 3 minutes.
- Now add ground beef and cook for about 5 more minutes or until the color has turned brown.
- Add potato, fish sauce, pepper, beef bouillon, water and some

salt into the pan and cook at low heat for 30 minutes while stirring regularly.

- Serve.

Serving: 6

Timing Information:

Preparation	Cooking	Total Time
20 mins	45 mins	1 hr 5 mins

Nutritional Information:

Calories	233 kcal
Carbohydrates	16.9 g
Cholesterol	46 mg
Fat	11.5 g
Fiber	2.4 g
Protein	15.4 g
Sodium	862 mg

* Percent Daily Values are based on a 2,000 calorie diet.

FISH SINIGANG

(TILAPIA)

Ingredients

- 1/2 pound tilapia fillets, cut into chunks
- 1 small head bok choy, chopped
- 2 medium tomatoes, cut into chunks
- 1 cup thinly sliced daikon radish
- 1/4 cup tamarind paste
- 3 cups water
- 2 dried red chile peppers(optional)

Directions

- Combine tilapia, radish, tomatoes, mixture of tamarind paste and water, chili peppers and bok choy.
- Bring the mixture to boil and cook for 5 minutes to get fish tender.
- Serve in appropriate bowls.

Serving: 10

Timing Information:

Preparation	Cooking	Total Time
5 mins	10 mins	15 mins

Nutritional Information:

Calories	112 kcal
Carbohydrates	13.4 g
Cholesterol	21 mg
Fat	1 g
Fiber	2.1 g
Protein	13.1 g
Sodium	63 mg

* Percent Daily Values are based on a 2,000 calorie diet.

Paksiw na Pata

(Pig's Feet Stew)

Ingredients

- 3 1/4 pounds pig's feet, rinsed and patted dry
- 1 1/2 cups vinegar
- 1 1/2 cups water
- 1/3 cup soy sauce
- 1 onion, diced
- 2 cloves garlic, crushed
- 1 tbsp whole black peppercorns, crushed
- 3 bay leaves
- 1 tbsp white sugar
- salt to taste

Directions

- Mix all the ingredients mentioned above in a pan and bring this mixture to boil for 3 minutes before turning the heat lower to medium and cooking for one full hour.
- Serve.

Serving: 5

Timing Information:

Preparation	Cooking	Total Time
10 mins	1hr 10 mins	1 hr 20 mins

Nutritional Information:

Calories	342 kcal
Carbohydrates	9.2 g
Cholesterol	138 mg
Fat	20.8 g
Fiber	1.2 g
Protein	30 g
Sodium	1061 mg

* Percent Daily Values are based on a 2,000 calorie diet.

Sinigang Na Baka

(Beef Based Veggie Soup)

Ingredients

- 2 tbsps canola oil
- 1 large onion, chopped
- 2 cloves garlic, chopped
- 1 pound beef stew meat, cut into 1 inch cubes
- 1 quart water
- 2 large tomatoes, diced
- 1/2 pound fresh green beans, rinsed and trimmed
- 1/2 medium head bok choy, cut into 1 1/2 inch strips
- 1 head fresh broccoli, cut into bite size pieces
- 1 (1.41 ounce) package tamarind soup base

Directions

- Cook onion and garlic in hot oil and then add beef to get it brown.
- Now add some water and bring it to a boil.

- Turn the heat down to medium and cook for 30 minutes.
- Cook for another 10 minutes after adding tomatoes and green beans.
- Now add tamarind soup mix, bok choy and some broccoli into the mix and cook for 10 more minutes to get everything tender.

Serving: 6
Timing Information:

Preparation	Cooking	Total Time
15 mins	45 mins	1 hr

Nutritional Information:

Calories	304 kcal
Carbohydrates	15 g
Cholesterol	51 mg
Fat	19.7 g
Fiber	4.5 g
Protein	17.8 g
Sodium	1405 mg

* Percent Daily Values are based on a 2,000 calorie diet.

MELON CHILLER

Ingredients

- 1 cantaloupe, halved and seeded
- 1 gallon water
- 2 cups white sugar
- ice cubes, as needed

Directions

- Take out the meat of cantaloupe and place into a punch bowl with a melon baller add sugar and some water after placing this into bowl.
- Mix it well and serve it cold.

Serving: 6

Timing Information:

Preparation	Cooking	Total Time
20 mins		1 hr 5 mins

Nutritional Information:

Calories	174 kcal
Carbohydrates	44.5 g
Cholesterol	0 mg
Fat	0.1 g
Fiber	0.5 g
Protein	0.5 g
Sodium	23 mg

* Percent Daily Values are based on a 2,000 calorie diet.

FILIPINO CHICKEN STEW

Ingredients

- 2 tbsps sesame oil
- 2 pounds boneless chicken pieces, cut into strips
- 2 tbsps fresh lemon juice
- 2 tbsps soy sauce
- 2 (15 ounce) cans coconut milk
- 1/4 cup red curry paste
- 1/4 cup flour
- 2 red bell peppers, chopped
- 1 sweet onion, chopped
- 1 red onion, chopped
- 2 cloves garlic, minced
- 2 large potatoes, cubed
- 2 (8 ounce) cans sliced bamboo shoots, drained
- 2 (8 ounce) cans sliced water chestnuts, drained
- 2 (8 ounce) cans baby corn, drained
- 1 (12 ounce) can sliced mushrooms, drained
- 1/4 cup chopped cilantro

Directions

- Cook chicken, lemon juice, and soy sauce in hot sesame oil over medium heat for 5 minutes and in a bowl mix flour, coconut milk and curry paste, and add this mixture to the pan.
- Now put bell pepper, red onion, garlic, potatoes, bamboo shoots, water chestnuts, sweet onion and mushrooms into the pan and cook at low heat for 45 minutes before adding cilantro and removing it from heat.
- Serve

Serving: 8

Timing Information:

Preparation	Cooking	Total Time
25 mins	50 mins	1 hr 15 mins

Nutritional Information:

Calories	554 kcal
Carbohydrates	28.4 g
Cholesterol	57 mg
Fat	32.3 g
Fiber	11.7 g
Protein	28.4 g
Sodium	645 mg

* Percent Daily Values are based on a 2,000 calorie diet.

CHAMPORADO

Ingredients

- 1 cup glutinous sweet rice
- 2 cups light coconut milk
- 1/2 cup cocoa powder
- 1 cup white sugar
- 1 tsp salt
- 1 cup thick coconut milk

Directions

- Bring the mixture of sweet rice and coconut milk to boil for 10 minutes while stirring regularly.
- Now add sugar, salt and cocoa power into this rice and cook at low heat for about 10 minutes or until you see that the rice is tender.
- Pour thick coconut milk into it and serve.

Serving: 8

Timing Information:

Preparation	Cooking	Total Time
5 mins	30 mins	35 mins

Nutritional Information:

Calories	428 kcal
Carbohydrates	53.4 g
Cholesterol	0 mg
Fat	25.2 g
Fiber	4.3 g
Protein	4.9 g
Sodium	407 mg

* Percent Daily Values are based on a 2,000 calorie diet.

Maja Blanca Maiz

(Corn Pudding)

Ingredients

- 1 2/3 cups coconut milk
- 1 (14.5 ounce) can cream-style corn
- 1 cup rice flour
- 1 cup white sugar

Directions

- Mix all the ingredients mentioned above thoroughly in a pan over medium heat and cook for 30 minutes or until the required thickness is achieved.
- Now pour everything into a serving platter and let it cool.
- Serve.

Serving: 10

Timing Information:

Preparation	Cooking	Total Time
5 mins	30 mins	1 hr 35 mins

Nutritional Information:

Calories	239 kcal
Carbohydrates	41.1 g
Cholesterol	0 mg
Fat	8.4 g
Fiber	1.3 g
Protein	2.4 g
Sodium	121 mg

* Percent Daily Values are based on a 2,000 calorie diet.

CASSAVA CAKE

Ingredients

- 2 cups grated, peeled yucca
- 2 eggs, beaten
- 1 (12 ounce) can evaporated milk
- 1 (14 ounce) can sweetened condensed milk
- 1 (14 ounce) can coconut milk

Directions

- Set your oven to 350 degrees F before continuing.
- Mix all the ingredients mentioned above in a bowl and pour this mixture into a baking dish.
- Bake this for one hour before switching on the broiler and letting it turn the top of the cake brown.
- Refrigerate before serving.

Serving: 1

Timing Information:

Preparation	Cooking	Total Time
20 mins	1 hr	2 hr 20 mins

Nutritional Information:

Calories	329 kcal
Carbohydrates	41.6 g
Cholesterol	60 mg
Fat	15.5 g
Fiber	1.2 g
Protein	8 g
Sodium	111 mg

* Percent Daily Values are based on a 2,000 calorie diet.

BUTTER COOKIES IN THE PHILIPPINES

Ingredients

- 1 cup butter, softened
- 1 cup white sugar
- 3 eggs
- 3 2/3 cups cornstarch
- 1 tsp cream of tartar
- 1 tsp baking powder

Directions

- Set your oven at 350 degrees F and grease the cookie sheets before continuing.
- Mix butter and sugar, and then add eggs one by one.
- Now add cornstarch, cream of tartar and some baking powder.
- Mix them well and place 1 inch balls over the greased cookie sheets.
- Bake this for 12 minutes in the preheated oven and then let it cool down before serving.

Serving: 5 dozen

Timing Information:

Preparation	Cooking	Total Time
5 mins	12 mins	17 mins

Nutritional Information:

Calories	74 kcal
Carbohydrates	10.5 g
Cholesterol	17 mg
Fat	3.3 g
Fiber	0.1 g
Protein	0.4 g
Sodium	34 mg

* Percent Daily Values are based on a 2,000 calorie diet.

FILIPINO MELON DESSERT II

Ingredients

- 4 pounds cantaloupe, shredded
- 1 (12 fluid ounce) can of evaporated milk
- 2 quarts water
- 1 1/4 cups white sugar

Directions

- Mix all the ingredients mentioned above thoroughly and then refrigerate for some time.
- Divide this into molds and freeze this for about 6 hours or until it is firm enough.

Serving: 20

Timing Information:

Preparation	Cooking	Total Time
15 mins		6 hr 15 mins

Nutritional Information:

Calories	105 kcal
Carbohydrates	21.8 g
Cholesterol	5 mg
Fat	1.6 g
Fiber	0.8 g
Protein	2 g
Sodium	37 mg

* Percent Daily Values are based on a 2,000 calorie diet.

CHOCOLATE-ORANGE RICE PUDDING

Ingredients

- 5 1/2 cups milk
- 1 cup Arborio rice
- 2/3 cup white sugar
- 2 tbsps orange juice
- 1 1/2 tsps grated orange zest
- 2 tbsps orange liqueur
- 1 tbsp unsweetened cocoa powder
- 1 cup semisweet chocolate chips

Directions

- Mix rice, orange zest, milk and orange juice in a pan and bring it to a boil before turning down the heat to medium and cooking for another 40 minutes or until the rice is tender.
- Add orange liqueur and cocoa powder into the rice mixture after removing it from the heat.
- Also add some chocolate chips and let it melt.

- Serve.

Serving: 8

Timing Information:

Preparation	Cooking	Total Time
10 mins	40 mins	50 mins

Nutritional Information:

Calories	356 kcal
Carbohydrates	60.6 g
Cholesterol	13 mg
Fat	9.7 g
Fiber	1.8 g
Protein	8.3 g
Sodium	72 mg

* Percent Daily Values are based on a 2,000 calorie diet.

GARLIC RICE

Ingredients

- 2 tbsps vegetable oil
- 1 1/2 tbsps chopped garlic
- 2 tbsps ground pork
- 4 cups cooked white rice
- 1 1/2 tsps garlic salt
- ground black pepper to taste

Directions

- Cook garlic and ground pork in hot oil over medium heat until golden brown.
- Now add cooked white rice and add some garlic and pepper according to your taste.
- Cook for about 3 minutes to get it mixed thoroughly.
- Serve.

Serving: 8

Timing Information:

Preparation	Cooking	Total Time
5 mins	5 mins	10 mins

Nutritional Information:

Calories	293 kcal
Carbohydrates	45.9 g
Cholesterol	6 mg
Fat	9 g
Fiber	0.8 g
Protein	5.9 g
Sodium	686 mg

* Percent Daily Values are based on a 2,000 calorie diet.

Corned Beef Hash In the Philippines

Ingredients

- 1 tbsp vegetable oil
- 4 cloves garlic, chopped
- 1 onion, diced
- 1 tomato, chopped
- 1 large potato, diced
- 1 (12 ounce) can corned beef
- salt and pepper to taste

Directions

- Cook onion and garlic over in hot oil over medium heat and then add tomatoes and potatoes.
- Cook for 10 minutes and then add beef, and cook for another 10 minutes.
- Add some salt and pepper before serving.
- Enjoy.

Serving: 4

Timing Information:

Preparation	Cooking	Total Time
15 mins	30 mins	45 mins

Nutritional Information:

Calories	333 kcal
Carbohydrates	21.1 g
Cholesterol	72 mg
Fat	16.2 g
Fiber	2.8 g
Protein	25.5 g
Sodium	853 mg

* Percent Daily Values are based on a 2,000 calorie diet.

CORNED BEEF WAFFLES

Ingredients

- 2 eggs
- 1 1/4 cups milk
- 2 tsps cooking oil
- 1 1/2 cups all-purpose flour
- 1 pinch salt
- 2 tsps baking powder
- 1/2 (12 ounce) can corned beef, broken into pieces

Directions

- Heat a waffle iron before continuing.
- Combine milk, oil and eggs in a bowl and in a separate bowl mix flour salt and baking powder.
- Combine both mixtures and add beef.
- Put this mixture into the preheated waffle iron and cook it until the waffles are golden in color.
- Serve it with butter.

Serving: 10

Timing Information:

Preparation	Cooking	Total Time
10 mins	10 mins	20 mins

Nutritional Information:

Calories	148 kcal
Carbohydrates	16 g
Cholesterol	54 mg
Fat	5.2 g
Fiber	0.5 g
Protein	8.8 g
Sodium	268 mg

* Percent Daily Values are based on a 2,000 calorie diet.

Mango Bread

Ingredients

- 2 cups all-purpose flour
- 2 tsps ground cinnamon
- 2 tsps baking soda
- 1/2 tsp salt
- 1 1/4 cups white sugar
- 2 eggs
- 3/4 cup vegetable oil
- 2 1/2 cups mangos, peeled, seeded and chopped
- 1 tsp lemon juice
- 1/4 cup raisins

Directions

- Mix all the dry ingredients mentioned above and then add eggs beaten in oil to this mixture.
- Now add mangoes, raisins and lemon.
- Pour this into two different pans and bake at 350 degrees F for 60 minutes.
- Serve.

Serving: 2

Timing Information:

Preparation	Cooking	Total Time
20 mins	1 hr	1 hr 20 mins

Nutritional Information:

Calories	193 kcal
Carbohydrates	27.2 g
Cholesterol	19 mg
Fat	8.9 g
Fiber	0.9 g
Protein	2.1 g
Sodium	192 mg

* Percent Daily Values are based on a 2,000 calorie diet.

Barbecued Pork Kebabs

Ingredients

- 1 cup white sugar
- 1 cup soy sauce
- 1 onion, diced
- 5 cloves garlic, chopped
- 1 tsp ground black pepper
- 1 (4 pound) boneless pork loin, cut into 1 1/2-inch cubes
- 10 bamboo skewers, soaked in water for 30 minutes

Directions

- Mix sugar, black pepper, soy sauce, garlic and onion in an appropriate bowl.
- Refrigerate for about 2 hours after adding pork.
- Preheat the grill or grilling plate to a high heat and put some oil before progressing.
- Now cook skewers with pork on the preheated grill for about 5 minutes each side.
- Serve.

NOTE: If using a grilling plate increase the amount of cooking time until you find your meat completely cooked.

Serving: 10

Timing Information:

Preparation	Cooking	Total Time
15 mins	15 mins	2 hr 30 mins

Nutritional Information:

Calories	369 kcal
Carbohydrates	24.7 g
Cholesterol	88 mg
Fat	15.8 g
Fiber	0.7 g
Protein	31.1 g
Sodium	1508 mg

* Percent Daily Values are based on a 2,000 calorie diet.

Guinataan Hito

(Catfish)

Ingredients

- 2 tbsps cooking oil
- 1 onion, chopped
- 2 cloves garlic, crushed
- 4 (4 ounce) catfish fillets
- salt and pepper to taste
- 1 1/2 cups coconut milk

Directions

- Cook onion and garlic in hot oil for about 10 minutes and then add catfish, and cook for another 2 minutes.
- Now add coconut milk and cook for another 10 minutes or until the coconut milk gets oily.
- Serve with rice.

Serving: 4

Timing Information:

Preparation	Cooking	Total Time
10 mins	30 mins	40 mins

Nutritional Information:

Calories	388 kcal
Carbohydrates	5.4 g
Cholesterol	51 mg
Fat	33.2 g
Fiber	1.4 g
Protein	19.1 g
Sodium	64 mg

* Percent Daily Values are based on a 2,000 calorie diet.

FILIPINO PORK ADOBO

Ingredients

- 1 cup distilled white vinegar
- 1 cup soy sauce
- 1/2 cup ketchup
- 1 tbsp minced garlic
- 3 bay leaves
- 1 tsp fresh-ground black pepper
- 2 1/2 pounds lean pork, cut into 1 inch cubes
- 1 pound small green beans, trimmed (optional)

Directions

- Combine pork, bay leaves, vinegar, garlic, soy sauce and ketchup, and bring them to boil at high heat.
- Now turn down the heat to low and cook for another two and a half hours.
- If you are using green beans in this recipe then add them in the last hour to get them tender.
- Serve.

Serving: 6

Timing Information:

Preparation	Cooking	Total Time
20 mins	2 hr 30 mins	2 hr 50 mins

Nutritional Information:

Calories	337 kcal
Carbohydrates	14.4 g
Cholesterol	90 mg
Fat	15.5 g
Fiber	3.1 g
Protein	35.1 g
Sodium	2687 mg

* Percent Daily Values are based on a 2,000 calorie diet.

BUKO II

(FILIPINO COCONUT PIE DESSERT)

Ingredients

- 1 fresh young coconut, drained with meat removed and chopped
- 2 (12 fluid ounce) cans of evaporated milk
- 1 (14 ounce) can sweetened condensed milk
- 4 eggs, beaten
- 1/4 cup white sugar
- 1 pinch salt

Directions

- Set your oven to 350 degrees F before continuing.
- Now combine all the ingredients mentioned above in a large bowl and pour into a baking dish.
- Fill the baking with enough water to cover half.

- Now bake everything in the preheated oven for about 60 minutes.
- Cool it down and serve.

Serving: 6

Timing Information:

Preparation	Cooking	Total Time
20 mins	1 hr	1 hr 50 mins

Nutritional Information:

Calories	693 kcal
Carbohydrates	66.9 g
Cholesterol	183 mg
Fat	40.7 g
Fiber	6 g
Protein	20.1 g
Sodium	276 mg

* Percent Daily Values are based on a 2,000 calorie diet.

CHAPTER 5: INDONESIA

INDONESIAN CLASSICAL SATAY

Ingredients

- 3 tbsps soy sauce
- 3 tbsps tomato sauce
- 1 tbsp peanut oil
- 2 cloves garlic, peeled and minced
- 1 pinch ground black pepper
- 1 pinch ground cumin
- 6 skinless, boneless chicken breast halves - cubed
- 1 tbsp vegetable oil
- 1/4 cup minced onion
- 1 clove garlic, peeled and minced
- 1 cup water
- 1/2 cup chunky peanut butter
- 2 tbsps soy sauce
- 2 tbsps white sugar
- 1 tbsp lemon juice

- skewers

Directions

- At first you need to set a grill or grilling plate to high heat and put some oil before starting anything else.
- Coat chicken with a mixture of soy sauce, cumin, tomato sauce, black pepper, peanut oil and garlic, and refrigerate it for at least 15 minutes.
- Cook onion and garlic in hot oil until brown before adding water, sugar, peanut butter and soy sauce into it.
- Add lemon juice after removing from heat.
- Thread all the chicken pieces into skewers
- Cook this on the preheated grill for about 5 minutes each side or until tender.
- Serve this with peanut sauce.

NOTE: If using a grilling plate please adjust the cooking time of the meat, to make sure that everything is cooked fully through.

NOTE: For peanut sauce recipe please see recipe for Satay Ayam.

NOTE: You will find that a few of these recipes call for a grill. Real Southeast Asian food is cooked street-style over an open flame, outside. For maximum authenticity use a grill.

Serving: 6

Timing Information:

Preparation	Cooking	Total Time
25 mins	20 mins	1 hr

Nutritional Information:

Calories	329 kcal
Carbohydrates	11.8 g
Cholesterol	67 mg
Fat	18.2 g
Fiber	2.2 g
Protein	30.8 g
Sodium	957 mg

* Percent Daily Values are based on a 2,000 calorie diet.

PORK SATAY

Ingredients

- 2 cloves garlic
- 1/2 cup chopped green onions
- 1 tbsp chopped fresh ginger root
- 1 cup roasted, salted Spanish peanuts
- 2 tbsps lemon juice
- 2 tbsps honey
- 1/2 cup soy sauce
- 2 tsps crushed coriander seed
- 1 tsp red pepper flakes
- 1/2 cup chicken broth
- 1/2 cup melted butter
- 1 1/2 pounds pork tenderloin, cut into 1 inch cubes
- skewers

Directions

- At first you need to set a grill or grilling plate to medium heat and put some oil before starting anything else.

- Blend garlic, ginger, soy sauce, peanuts, lemon juice, honey, green onions, coriander, and red pepper flakes in a blender until you see that a smoothness is achieved.

- Coat pork cubes with this mixture by placing everything in a plastic bag and refrigerating for at least six hours.

- Thread pork cubes taken out from the bag onto skewers and boil the remaining marinade for about 5 minutes

- Cook this on the preheated grill for about 15 minutes each side or until tender, while brushing frequently with the cooked marinade.

- Serve with the remaining marinade.

NOTE: If using a grilling plate please adjust the cooking time of the meat, to make sure that everything is cooked fully through.

Serving: 4

Timing Information:

Preparation	Cooking	Total Time
30 mins	10 mins	6 hr 40 mins

Nutritional Information:

Calories	683 kcal
Carbohydrates	22.1 g
Cholesterol	156 mg
Fat	49.7 g
Fiber	4.2 g
Protein	41.6 g
Sodium	2332 mg

* Percent Daily Values are based on a 2,000 calorie diet.

INDO-CHINESE SPICED RICE

Ingredients

- 3 tbsps vegetable oil
- 1 large onion, chopped
- 2 jalapeno peppers, seeded and minced
- 2 cloves garlic, crushed
- 1 tsp ground turmeric
- 1/2 tsp ground cinnamon
- 2 cups uncooked long-grain white rice
- 2 (14.5 ounce) cans chicken broth
- 1 cup water
- 1 bay leaf
- 2 green onions, chopped

Directions

- Cook onion, garlic and jalapeno peppers for about eight minutes before adding turmeric and cooking for two more minutes.

- Now add chicken broth, bay leaf and water, and cook all this for about 20 minutes after bringing this mixture to boil.
- Turn the heat off and let it stand as it is for about five minutes.
- Sprinkle some green onion over it before serving.

Serving: 8

Timing Information:

Preparation	Cooking	Total Time
10 mins	25 mins	35 mins

Nutritional Information:

Calories	226 kcal
Carbohydrates	39.8 g
Cholesterol	0 mg
Fat	5.5 g
Fiber	1.3 g
Protein	3.7 g
Sodium	4 mg

* Percent Daily Values are based on a 2,000 calorie diet.

Nasi Goreng

(Chicken Fried Rice Dish with Sauce)

Ingredients

- 12 ounces long grain white rice
- 3 cups water
- salt to taste
- 2 tbsps sunflower seed oil
- 1 pound skinless, boneless chicken breast halves
- 2 cloves garlic, coarsely chopped
- 1 fresh red chile pepper, seeded and chopped
- 1 tbsp curry paste
- 1 bunch green onions, thinly sliced
- 2 tbsps soy sauce, or more to taste
- 1 tsp sunflower seed oil
- 2 eggs
- 2 ounces roasted peanuts, coarsely chopped

- 1/4 cup chopped fresh cilantro

Directions

- Bring a mixture of rice, water and salt to boil in a pan before turning down the heat to low and cooking for another 25 minutes to get the rice tender.
- Cook chicken, garlic and red chili pepper for about seven minutes before adding curry paste, cooked rice and green onion into it and cooking for another five minutes, while adding soy sauce at the end.
- Put the rice mixture aside; cook egg in the in a pot and when finished, mix it with the rice very thoroughly.
- Garnish with peanuts and cilantro before serving.

Serving: 6

Timing Information:

Preparation	Cooking	Total Time
15 mins	35 mins	50 mins

Nutritional Information:

Calories	430 kcal
Carbohydrates	51.5 g
Cholesterol	101 mg
Fat	13.8 g
Fiber	2.7 g
Protein	24.3 g
Sodium	491 mg

* Percent Daily Values are based on a 2,000 calorie diet.

Indonesian Inspired Ketchup

Ingredients

- 1 1/4 cups soy sauce
- 1 cup molasses (such as Grandma's®)
- 2 tbsps brown sugar
- 1 cube chicken bouillon (such as Knorr®)

Directions

- Mix all the ingredients mentioned above in a saucepan and cook it over low heat until you see that a slow boil is reached.
- Turn the heat off and cool it down.
- Store this in an airtight container and in a refrigerator.

Serving: 3

Timing Information:

Preparation	Cooking	Total Time
5 mins	15 mins	20 mins

Nutritional Information:

Calories	31 kcal
Carbohydrates	7.4 g
Cholesterol	< 1 mg
Fat	0 g
Fiber	0.1 g
Protein	0.5 g
Sodium	479 mg

* Percent Daily Values are based on a 2,000 calorie diet.

INDONESIAN FRIED RICE

Ingredients

- 1/2 cup uncooked long grain white rice
- 1 cup water
- 2 tsps sesame oil
- 1 small onion, chopped
- 2 cloves garlic, minced
- 1 green chile pepper, chopped
- 1 small carrot, sliced
- 1 stalk celery, sliced
- 2 tbsps kecap manis
- 2 tbsps tomato sauce
- 2 tbsps soy sauce
- 1/4 cucumber, sliced
- 4 eggs

Directions

- Bring a mixture of rice and water to boil before turning down the heat to low and cooking for 20 minutes.

- Cook onion, green chili and garlic in hot oil for a few minutes before adding carrot, rice, tomato sauce, celery, soy sauce and kecap manis, and cooking for another few minutes.
- Transfer this to a bowl, while garnishing with cucumber slices.
- Cook eggs in the pan and when done, put them over rice and vegetables.

Serving: 4

Timing Information:

Preparation	Cooking	Total Time
25 mins	15 mins	40 mins

Nutritional Information:

Calories	215 kcal
Carbohydrates	26.7 g
Cholesterol	186 mg
Fat	7.7 g
Fiber	1.6 g
Protein	10 g
Sodium	1033 mg

* Percent Daily Values are based on a 2,000 calorie diet.

INDO-CHINESE CHICKEN

Ingredients

- 1 cup uncooked long grain white rice
- 2 cups water
- 1 pound fresh green beans, trimmed and snapped
- 2 tsps olive oil
- 1 pound skinless, boneless chicken breast halves - cut into chunks
- 3/4 cup low-sodium chicken broth
- 1/3 cup smooth peanut butter
- 2 tsps honey
- 1 tbsp low sodium soy sauce
- 1 tsp red chile paste
- 2 tbsps lemon juice
- 3 green onions, thinly sliced
- 2 tbsps chopped peanuts(optional)

Directions

- Bring a mixture of rice and water to boil before turning down the heat to low and cooking for 20 minutes.
- Put green beans in a steamer basket over boiling water and steam it for about ten minutes or until you find that it is tender.
- Cook chicken in hot oil for about five minutes on each side.
- Combine chicken broth, honey, soy sauce, peanut butter, chile paste and lemon juice in a pan, and cook it for about five minutes before adding green beans.
- Serve this over rice and garnish with green onions and peanuts.

Serving: 4

Timing Information:

Preparation	Cooking	Total Time
15 mins	30 mins	45 mins

Nutritional Information:

Calories	530 kcal
Carbohydrates	58.1 g
Cholesterol	59 mg
Fat	18.6 g
Fiber	6.4 g
Protein	35.4 g
Sodium	322 mg

* Percent Daily Values are based on a 2,000 calorie diet.

MIE GORENG

(INDONESIAN FRIED NOODLES)

Ingredients

- 3 (3 ounce) packages ramen noodles (without flavor packets)
- 1 tbsp vegetable oil
- 1 pound skinless, boneless chicken breast halves, cut into strips
- 1 tsp olive oil
- 1 tsp garlic salt
- 1 pinch ground black pepper, or to taste
- 1 tbsp vegetable oil
- 1/2 cup chopped shallots
- 5 cloves garlic, chopped
- 1 cup shredded cabbage
- 1 cup shredded carrots
- 1 cup broccoli florets
- 1 cup sliced fresh mushrooms
- 1/4 cup soy sauce

- 1/4 cup sweet soy sauce (Indonesian kecap manis)
- 1/4 cup oyster sauce
- salt and pepper to taste

Directions

- Cook noodles in boiling water for about 3 minutes before running it through cold water to stop the process of cooking and draining all the water.
- Coat chicken strips with olive oil, black pepper and garlic salt before cooking it in hot oil for about 5 minutes or until you see that the chicken is no longer pink.
- Now add garlic and shallots, and cook them until you see that they are turning brown.
- Now add all the vegetables into the pan and cook it for another five minutes or until you see that the vegetables are tender.
- Add the mixture of noodles, soy sauce, oyster sauce and sweet soy

sauce into the pan containing chicken and vegetables.

- Sprinkle some salt and pepper before serving.
- Enjoy.

Serving: 6

Timing Information:

Preparation	Cooking	Total Time
15 mins	25 mins	40 mins

Nutritional Information:

Calories	356 kcal
Carbohydrates	34 g
Cholesterol	43 mg
Fat	14.3 g
Fiber	1.7 g
Protein	22.7 g
Sodium	1824 mg

* Percent Daily Values are based on a 2,000 calorie diet.

PISANG GORENG

(INDONESIAN BANANA FRITTERS I)

Ingredients

- 1 1/4 cups all-purpose flour
- 2 tbsps granulated sugar
- 1/4 tbsp vanilla powder
- 1/2 cup milk
- 1 egg
- 2 tbsps butter, melted
- 1 tsp rum flavoring
- 4 ripe bananas, sliced
- 2 cups oil for frying

Directions

- Mix flour, vanilla powder and sugar before making a space in the center and adding milk, melted butter, egg and rum flavoring.

- Combine it thoroughly before adding banana slices.
- Fry this banana mixture in hot oil for about 15 minutes or until golden brown.
- Remove these bananas from the oil and drain it well with the help of paper towels.
- Serve.

Serving: 4

Timing Information:

Preparation	Cooking	Total Time
5 mins	15 mins	20 mins

Nutritional Information:

Calories	489 kcal
Carbohydrates	73.2 g
Cholesterol	64 mg
Fat	19.5 g
Fiber	5 g
Protein	8.3 g
Sodium	73 mg

* Percent Daily Values are based on a 2,000 calorie diet.

Kecap Manis Sedang

(Indo-Chinese Soy Sauce)

Ingredients

- 2/3 cup soy sauce
- 1 cup water
- 2/3 cup brown sugar
- 8 bay leaves

Directions

- In a mixture of sugar, water and soy sauce in a saucepan, put bay leaves and bring all this to a boil.
- Now turn down the heat to medium and cook it for another 30 minutes.
- Let cool.

NOTE: This recipe is very important for multiple Indonesian and Indo-Chinese dishes mentioned throughout this cookbook.

Serving: 12

Timing Information:

Preparation	Cooking	Total Time
5 mins	15 mins	20 mins

Nutritional Information:

Calories	54 kcal
Carbohydrates	13.1 g
Cholesterol	0 mg
Fat	0 g
Fiber	0.1 g
Protein	0.9 g
Sodium	806 mg

* Percent Daily Values are based on a 2,000 calorie diet.

Satay Ayam

(Indo chicken with Peanut Sauce)

Ingredients

- 1 pound chicken thighs, cut into 1/2-inch pieces
- 3/4 tsp salt
- 1 pinch ground white pepper
- 1 tbsp sunflower seed oil
- 24 wooden skewers

Peanut Sauce:

- 1 cup water
- 5 tbsps peanut butter
- 2 tbsps kecap manis (sweet soy sauce)
- 1 tbsp brown sugar
- 2 cloves garlic, minced
- 1/2 tsp salt
- 1 tbsp lime juice

Directions

- Coat chicken thighs with ¾ tsp salt, sunflower seed oil and white pepper before refrigerating it for at least two hours.
- Bring a mixture of water, salt, peanut butter, kecap manis, garlic and brown sugar to boil before removing it from heat and adding some lime juice to make peanut sauce.
- Thread these chicken thighs onto skewers, while saving some marinade for later use.
- Cook these chicken thighs on a preheated grill for about 2 minutes each side or until tender.
- Serve this with peanut sauce.

NOTE: You can use a grilling plate as well for this recipe, just increase the cooking time of the meat. Use of a grill is preferred.

Serving: 4

Timing Information:

Preparation	Cooking	Total Time
10 mins	30 mins	40 mins

Nutritional Information:

Calories	326 kcal
Carbohydrates	8.9 g
Cholesterol	70 mg
Fat	21.8 g
Fiber	1.4 g
Protein	24.9 g
Sodium	1339 mg

* Percent Daily Values are based on a 2,000 calorie diet.

Skirt Steak

Ingredients

- 1 1/2 cups sweet soy sauce (Indonesian kecap manis)
- 1 cup sake
- 1 cup pineapple juice
- 1 cup mirin
- 1/2 cup reduced-sodium soy sauce
- 1/4 bunch fresh cilantro, chopped
- 1 tbsp white sugar
- 1 tbsp minced fresh ginger root
- 1 tbsp minced garlic
- 1 tbsp chopped scallions (green onions)
- 1 tbsp chili paste(optional)
- 1 (1 pound) skirt steak

Directions

- At first you need to set grill or grilling plate to medium heat and put some oil before starting anything else.

- Mix sweet soy sauce (kecap manis), scallions, sake, mirin, reduced-sodium soy sauce, cilantro, pineapple juice, sugar, ginger, garlic, and chili paste in large sized glass bowl before coating skirt steak with this mixture.
- Wrap it up with a plastic bag and marinate it for at least three hours.
- Remove every piece of meat from the marinade and cook this marinade in a saucepan for about 10 minutes over medium heat.
- Cook meat on the preheated grill for about 8 minutes each side or until tender.
- Serve it with the cooked marinade.

NOTE: If using a grilling plate please adjust the cooking time of the meat, to

make sure that everything is cooked
fully through.

Serving: 6

Timing Information:

Preparation	Cooking	Total Time
15 mins	20 mins	35 mins

Nutritional Information:

Calories	437 kcal
Carbohydrates	46.2 g
Cholesterol	27 mg
Fat	4.8 g
Fiber	1.4 g
Protein	22.5 g
Sodium	6517 mg

* Percent Daily Values are based on a 2,000 calorie diet.

Prawn Nasi Goreng

(Fried Rice and Shrimp In Sauce)

Ingredients

- 2 tbsps vegetable oil, divided
- 3 eggs, beaten
- 2 tbsps dark soy sauce
- 2 tbsps ketchup
- 1 tbsp brown sugar
- 1 tsp toasted sesame oil
- 1 tsp sweet chili sauce
- 1 zucchini, chopped
- 1 carrot, chopped
- 8 green onions, sliced
- 1 clove garlic, crushed
- 2 cups cooked rice
- 1/2 pound cooked prawns
- 2 tbsps fresh chives, chopped

Directions

- Cook egg in hot oil for about 30 seconds each side and cut it into smaller pieces after letting it cool down.
- Mix soy sauce, brown sugar, sesame oil, ketchup and chili sauce in a bowl, and set it aside for later use.
- Cook zucchini, green onions and carrot in hot oil for about three minutes before adding garlic, sauce mixture, rice and prawns.
- Turn the heat off and serve it by topping with eggs and sliced chives.

Serving: 2

Timing Information:

Preparation	Cooking	Total Time
20 mins	10 mins	30 mins

Nutritional Information:

Calories	664 kcal
Carbohydrates	67.7 g
Cholesterol	500 mg
Fat	25.5 g
Fiber	4 g
Protein	41 g
Sodium	1497 mg

* Percent Daily Values are based on a 2,000 calorie diet.

JEMPUT JUMPUT

(INDO BANANA FRITTERS II)

Ingredients

- 5/8 cup all-purpose flour
- 1 pinch salt
- 1 tsp baking powder
- 6 ripe bananas
- 3 tbsps white sugar
- oil for frying

Directions

- Add a mixture of baking powder, flour and salt slowly into mashed bananas and sugar, while stirring continuously.
- Drop this mixture with help of a spoon into hot oil and cook for about 8 minutes, while turning only once.
- Serve after draining with paper towels.

Serving: 18

Timing Information:

Preparation	Cooking	Total Time
10 mins	15 mins	25 mins

Nutritional Information:

Calories	491 kcal
Carbohydrates	14.4 g
Cholesterol	0 mg
Fat	49.1 g
Fiber	1.1 g
Protein	0.9 g
Sodium	49 mg

* Percent Daily Values are based on a 2,000 calorie diet.

CHICKEN & BROCCOLI

Ingredients

- 12 ounces boneless, skinless chicken breast halves, cut into bite-sized pieces
- 1 tbsp oyster sauce
- 2 tbsps dark soy sauce
- 3 tbsps vegetable oil
- 2 cloves garlic, chopped
- 1 large onion, cut into rings
- 1/2 cup water
- 1 tsp ground black pepper
- 1 tsp white sugar
- 1/2 medium head bok choy, chopped
- 1 small head broccoli, chopped
- 1 tbsp cornstarch, mixed with equal parts water

Directions

- Mix chicken, soy sauce and oyster sauce in large bowl and set it aside for later use.
- Cook garlic and onion in hot oil for about three minutes before adding chicken mixture and cooking it for another ten minutes.
- Now add water, sugar, broccoli, pepper and bok choy, and cook it for another ten minutes.
- In the end, add cornstarch mixture and cook it for another 5 minutes to get the sauce thick.
- Enjoy.

Serving: 6

Timing Information:

Preparation	Cooking	Total Time
10 mins	25 mins	35 mins

Nutritional Information:

Calories	170 kcal
Carbohydrates	9.8 g
Cholesterol	33 mg
Fat	7.9 g
Fiber	2.5 g
Protein	16.2 g
Sodium	418 mg

* Percent Daily Values are based on a 2,000 calorie diet.

INDO-CHINESE SATE

(MEAT KABOBS)

Ingredients

- 1 onion, chopped
- 1 clove garlic, minced
- 1 1/2 tbsps kecap manis
- 1 tsp ground coriander
- 1 tsp ground cumin
- 1 tsp sambal oelek (sriracha sauce)
- 1/2 cup red wine
- 1 1/2 tbsps water
- 1 lemon grass, bruised, and cut into 1 inch pieces
- 1 pound sirloin steak, cut into 1-inch cubes

Directions

- At first you need to set a grill or grilling plate to medium heat and

put some oil before starting
anything else.

- Blend onion, garlic, coriander,
  cumin, kecap manis, sambal
  oelek, red wine and water in a
  blender until smooth before
  adding lemon grass and coating
  beef with this marinade.
- Wrap it up with a plastic bag and
  refrigerate it for at least two
  hours.
- Thread these beef pieces onto the
  skewers.
- Cook this on the preheated grill
  for about 5 minutes each side or
  until tender.

NOTE: If using a grilling plate please
adjust the cooking time of the meat, to
make sure that everything is cooked
fully through.

Serving: 4

Timing Information:

Preparation	Cooking	Total Time
15 mins	5 mins	2 hr 20 mins

Nutritional Information:

Calories	200 kcal
Carbohydrates	6.5 g
Cholesterol	69 mg
Fat	5.4 g
Fiber	0.9 g
Protein	25.1 g
Sodium	419 mg

* Percent Daily Values are based on a 2,000 calorie diet.

Telur Balado

(Spicy Indonesian Eggs)

Ingredients

- 1 cup vegetable oil for frying
- 6 hard-boiled eggs, shells removed
- 6 red chili peppers, seeded and chopped
- 4 cloves garlic
- 4 medium shallots
- 2 tomatoes, quartered
- 1 tsp shrimp paste
- 1 1/2 tbsps peanut oil
- 1 tbsp vegetable oil
- 1 tsp white vinegar
- 1 tsp white sugar
- salt and pepper to taste

Directions

- Deep fry eggs in a pan for about seven minutes over medium heat or until golden brown in color.
- Put chili peppers, shallots, garlic, tomatoes, and shrimp in a blender until you see that the required smoothness is achieved.
- Cook chili pepper mixture in hot oil before adding vinegar, pepper, sugar, fried eggs and salt into a mixture.
- Turn down the heat to medium and cook it for about 5 minutes, while turning it frequently.
- Serve.

Serving: 6

Timing Information:

Preparation	Cooking	Total Time
15 mins	20 mins	35 mins

Nutritional Information:

Calories	237 kcal
Carbohydrates	13.1 g
Cholesterol	201 mg
Fat	17.3 g
Fiber	1.4 g
Protein	9.1 g
Sodium	115 mg

* Percent Daily Values are based on a 2,000 calorie diet.

Ayam Masak Merah

(Spicy Tomato Chicken)

Ingredients

- 1 (3 pound) whole chicken, cut into 8 pieces
- 1 tsp ground turmeric
- salt to taste
- 1/4 cup dried red chili peppers
- 3 fresh red chili pepper, finely chopped
- 4 cloves garlic, minced
- 1 red onion, chopped
- 1 (3/4 inch thick) slice fresh ginger root
- 2 tbsps sunflower seed oil
- 1 cinnamon stick
- 2 whole star anise pods
- 5 whole cloves
- 5 cardamom seeds
- 2 tomatoes, sliced
- 2 tbsps ketchup
- 1 tsp white sugar, or to taste

- 1/2 cup water

Directions

- Coat chicken with turmeric powder and salt, and set it aside for later use.
- Put dried red chili peppers in hot water until you see that it is soft.
- Put softened dried chili, garlic, fresh red chili peppers, onion, and ginger in a blender and blend it until you get a paste.
- Cook chicken in hot oil until you see that it is golden from all sides and set it aside.
- Now cook chili paste, cinnamon, cardamom seeds, star anise, and cloves in the same pan for few minutes before adding chicken and water into it.
- Add tomatoes, sugar and ketchup, and bring all this to a boil before turning down the heat to medium and cooking for another 15 minutes.
- Serve.

Serving: 4

Timing Information:

Preparation	Cooking	Total Time
20 mins	35 mins	55 mins

Nutritional Information:

Calories	462 kcal
Carbohydrates	15.4 g
Cholesterol	92 mg
Fat	29.7 g
Fiber	3.3 g
Protein	33.6 g
Sodium	183 mg

* Percent Daily Values are based on a 2,000 calorie diet.

CAP CAI

(INDO-CHINESE SHRIMP VEGGIE SALAD)

Ingredients

- 3 tbsps vegetable oil
- 4 cloves garlic, minced
- 1 onion, thinly sliced
- 10 ounces peeled and deveined medium shrimp (30-40 per pound)
- 1 head bok choy, chopped
- 1 1/2 cups chopped broccoli
- 1 1/2 cups chopped cauliflower
- 1 large carrot, thinly sliced at an angle
- 3 green onions, chopped
- 2/3 cup water
- 2 tbsps cornstarch
- 2 tbsps fish sauce
- 2 tbsps oyster sauce
- 1 tsp white sugar

- 1/2 tsp ground black pepper
- salt to taste

Directions

- Cook onion and garlic in hot oil for about five minutes before adding shrimp, broccoli, cauliflower, bok choy, carrot, water and green onion, and cook this for about 15 minutes or until you see that all the vegetables are tender.
- Add a mixture of fish sauce and cornstarch, to the cap cai and also some oyster sauce, pepper and sugar.
- Mix it thoroughly and add some salt according to your taste before serving.

Serving: 4

Timing Information:

Preparation	Cooking	Total Time
20 mins	25 mins	45 mins

Nutritional Information:

Calories	250 kcal
Carbohydrates	18.7 g
Cholesterol	106 mg
Fat	11.9 g
Fiber	4.4 g
Protein	18.9 g
Sodium	819 mg

* Percent Daily Values are based on a 2,000 calorie diet.

A Southeast Asian Sandwich

Ingredients

- 4 boneless pork loin chops, cut 1/4 inch thick
- 4 (7 inch) French bread baguettes, split lengthwise
- 4 tsps mayonnaise, or to taste
- 1 ounce chile sauce with garlic (sriracha sauce)
- 1/4 cup fresh lime juice
- 1 small red onion, sliced into rings
- 1 medium cucumber, peeled and sliced lengthwise
- 2 tbsps chopped fresh cilantro
- salt and pepper to taste

Directions

- Put pork chops in a broiling pan and cook it for about 5 minutes or until you see that it is brown from each side.

- Put mayonnaise evenly on French rolls and also put one pork chop on each roll.
- Put chili sauce on the meat and add some lime juice, while topping it with onion, pepper, cucumber, salt and cilantro.
- Add some more lime juice just before serving.

Serving: 4

Timing Information:

Preparation	Cooking	Total Time
10 mins	5 mins	15 mins

Nutritional Information:

Calories	627 kcal
Carbohydrates	72.1 g
Cholesterol	124 mg
Fat	12.1 g
Fiber	3.3 g
Protein	55.3 g
Sodium	1005 mg

* Percent Daily Values are based on a 2,000 calorie diet.

Chapter 6: Vietnam

Chicken Meatballs In Vietnam

Ingredients

- 1 1/2 pounds ground chicken
- 1 clove garlic, minced
- 1 egg white
- 1 tbsp rice wine
- 2 tbsps soy sauce
- 1/2 tsp Worcestershire sauce
- 2 tsps fish sauce
- 1/2 tsp white sugar
- salt and white pepper to taste
- 2 tbsps cornstarch
- 1 tbsp sesame oil

Directions

- Preheat the broiler of your oven before doing anything else.

- Combine ground chicken, Worcestershire sauce, sugar, garlic, rice wine, soy sauce, egg white, fish sauce, salt, pepper, corn starch and sesame oil in a medium sized bowl before forming small balls out of it and threading them onto skewers.
- Put these skewers on a baking sheet.
- Broil it for 20 minutes or until you see that it is cooked.

Serving: 6

Timing Information:

Preparation	Cooking	Total Time
20 mins	35 mins	55 mins

Nutritional Information:

Calories	184 kcal
Carbohydrates	4.1 g
Cholesterol	69 mg
Fat	5.9 g
Fiber	0.1 g
Protein	26.5 g
Sodium	497 mg

* Percent Daily Values are based on a 2,000 calorie diet.

Spring Rolls Vietnamese Style

Ingredients

- 2 ounces rice vermicelli
- 8 rice wrappers (8.5 inch diameter)
- 8 large cooked shrimp - peeled, deveined and cut in half
- 1 1/3 tbsps chopped fresh Thai basil
- 3 tbsps chopped fresh mint leaves
- 3 tbsps chopped fresh cilantro
- 2 leaves lettuce, chopped
- 4 tsps fish sauce
- 1/4 cup water
- 2 tbsps fresh lime juice
- 1 clove garlic, minced
- 2 tbsps white sugar
- 1/2 tsp garlic chili sauce
- 3 tbsps hoisin sauce
- 1 tsp finely chopped peanuts

Directions

- Cook rice vermicelli in boiling water for five minutes or until done and then drain.
- Dip a rice wrapper in hot water for one second to soften it up before placing shrimp halves, basil, mint, vermicelli, cilantro and lettuce, and then roll this wrapper around these things.
- Mix fish sauce, lime juice, garlic, water, sugar and chili sauce in a small bowl before mixing peanuts and hoisin sauce in a separate bowl.
- Serve spring roll with these two sauces.

Serving: 8

Timing Information:

Preparation	Cooking	Total Time
45 mins	5 mins	50 mins

Nutritional Information:

Calories	82 kcal
Carbohydrates	15.8 g
Cholesterol	11 mg
Fat	0.7 g
Fiber	0.6 g
Protein	3.3 g
Sodium	305 mg

* Percent Daily Values are based on a 2,000 calorie diet.

A Vietnamese Inspired Chicken Salad

Ingredients

- 1 tbsp finely chopped green chile peppers
- 1 tbsp rice vinegar
- 2 tbsps fresh lime juice
- 3 tbsps Asian fish sauce
- 3 cloves garlic, minced
- 1 tbsp white sugar
- 1 tbsp Asian (toasted) sesame oil
- 2 tbsps vegetable oil
- 1 tsp black pepper
- 2 cooked skinless boneless chicken breast halves, shredded
- 1/2 head cabbage, cored and thinly sliced
- 1 carrot, cut into matchsticks
- 1/3 onion, finely chopped
- 1/3 cup finely chopped dry roasted peanuts
- 1/3 cup chopped fresh cilantro

Directions

- Combine chopped green chilies, sesame oil, lime juice, fish sauce, garlic, sugar, rice vinegar, vegetable oil and black pepper in a medium sized bowl very thoroughly so that the sugar is completely dissolved.
- Mix chicken, carrot, onion, peanuts, cabbage and cilantro in a separate bowl.
- Pour the bowl containing dressing over this and serve it after thoroughly mixing it.

Serving: 4

Timing Information:

Preparation	Cooking	Total Time
30 mins		30 mins

Nutritional Information:

Calories	303 kcal
Carbohydrates	19.3 g
Cholesterol	37 mg
Fat	17.9 g
Fiber	5.7 g
Protein	19.2 g
Sodium	991 mg

* Percent Daily Values are based on a 2,000 calorie diet.

Lamb Chops In Vietnam

Ingredients

- 15 (3 ounce) lamb loin chops (1-inch thick) lamb loin chops (1-inch thick)
- 2 cloves garlic, sliced
- 1 tsp garlic powder, or to taste
- 1 pinch chili powder
- 2 tbsps white sugar
- freshly ground black pepper to taste
- 1 tbsp fresh lime juice
- 1 tbsp soy sauce
- 2 tbsps olive oil
- 1/4 cup chopped fresh cilantro
- 2 lime wedges
- 2 lemon wedges

Directions

- Set your oven at 400 degrees F before doing anything else.

- Add the garlic, garlic powder, sugar, salt, lime juice, chili powder, soy sauce, olive oil and pepper in a roasting pan over lamb chops.
- Bake this in the preheated oven for about 30 minutes or until tender before garnishing it with cilantro and adding some lime juice.
- Serve.

Serving: 5

Timing Information:

Preparation	Cooking	Total Time
10 mins	20 mins	8 hr 30 mins

Nutritional Information:

Calories	555 kcal
Carbohydrates	7.4 g
Cholesterol	151 mg
Fat	40.4 g
Fiber	0.6 g
Protein	38.6 g
Sodium	301 mg

* Percent Daily Values are based on a 2,000 calorie diet.

A Southeast Asian Pork I

Ingredients

- 1 tbsp vegetable oil
- 1 cup white sugar
- 2 pounds pork spareribs, cut into 1-inch pieces
- 2 green onions, cut in 2-inch lengths
- 1 green chili pepper, chopped
- 1 tsp ground black pepper
- 2 shallots, finely chopped
- 2 cloves garlic, minced
- salt to taste
- 1 tsp Asian (toasted) sesame oil
- 1 tbsp green onion, thinly sliced and separated into rings

Directions

- Cook sugar in hot oil in a skillet until you see that it is turning brown in color before adding pork, 2 green onions, black pepper, chili pepper, shallots, garlic, and salt, and mixing all this very thoroughly in the caramelized sugar.

- After the pork turns golden brown; add sesame oil and vegetables into it before turning down the heat to low and cooking it for a few minutes.
- When you see that juices have been absorbed then turn up the heat to high and cook all this for five minutes or until you see that the sauce is thick enough.
- Garnish this with some green onion rings.
- Serve

Serving: 4

Timing Information:

Preparation	Cooking	Total Time
15 mins	20 mins	35 mins

Nutritional Information:

Calories	657 kcal
Carbohydrates	56.8 g
Cholesterol	120 mg
Fat	34.7 g
Fiber	0.7 g
Protein	29.9 g
Sodium	98 mg

* Percent Daily Values are based on a 2,000 calorie diet.

Pho Soup

Ingredients

- 2 (14.5 ounce) cans chicken broth
- 2 star anise pods, or more to taste
- 3/4 tbsp ginger paste
- 1 tsp sriracha hot sauce, or more to taste
- 4 ounces tofu, cubed
- 1/2 cup broccoli florets
- 1/2 cup sliced mushrooms
- 1/4 cup chopped carrots
- 1/2 (8 ounce) package dried thin rice noodles
- 1 tbsp chopped green onion

Directions

- Bring the mixture of chicken broth, ginger paste, star anise and sriracha hot sauce to boil before adding carrots, tofu, mushrooms and broccoli, and cooking it for seven minutes or until you see that the vegetables are tender.

- Put noodles in hot water for about four minutes and drain.
- After removing star anise from the broth mixture, add this mixture on top of noodles in serving bowls.
- Serve.

Serving: 4

Timing Information:

Preparation	Cooking	Total Time
15 mins	10 mins	25 mins

Nutritional Information:

Calories	159 kcal
Carbohydrates	29.2 g
Cholesterol	5 mg
Fat	2.3 g
Fiber	1.7 g
Protein	5.2 g
Sodium	991 mg

* Percent Daily Values are based on a 2,000 calorie diet.

SOUTHEAST ASIAN PORK II

Ingredients

- 4 pounds pork shoulder, cut into cubes
- 1 tsp salt
- 1 tsp ground black pepper
- 1/4 cup olive oil
- 2 cloves garlic, minced
- 2 tbsps brown sugar
- 2 tbsps soy sauce
- 1 tbsp fish sauce
- 1 tsp Chinese five-spice powder

Directions

- Cook garlic and pork that is seasoned with salt and pepper in hot oil for about ten minutes or until you see that pork is browned.
- Now add brown sugar, five-spice powder, soy sauce and fish sauce into the pork before turning down

the heat to low and cooking it for 2 full hours or until you see that pork is tender.

- Serve.

Serving: 4

Timing Information:

Preparation	Cooking	Total Time
10 mins	2 hr 20 mins	2 hr 30 mins

Nutritional Information:

Calories	288 kcal
Carbohydrates	4.4 g
Cholesterol	85 mg
Fat	16.4 g
Fiber	0.1 g
Protein	29.5
Sodium	713 mg

* Percent Daily Values are based on a 2,000 calorie diet.

Easy Vietnamese Inspired Stir-Fry

Ingredients

- 1/4 cup olive oil
- 4 cloves garlic, minced
- 1 (1 inch) piece fresh ginger root, minced
- 1/4 cup fish sauce
- 1/4 cup reduced-sodium soy sauce
- 1 dash sesame oil
- 2 pounds sirloin tip, thinly sliced
- 1 tbsp vegetable oil
- 2 cloves garlic, minced
- 3 green onions, cut into 2 inch pieces
- 1 large onion, thinly sliced
- 2 cups frozen whole green beans, partially thawed
- 1/2 cup reduced-sodium beef broth
- 2 tbsps lime juice
- 1 tbsp chopped fresh Thai basil

- 1 tbsp chopped fresh mint
- 1 pinch red pepper flakes, or to taste
- 1/2 tsp ground black pepper
- 1/4 cup chopped fresh cilantro

Directions

- Add a mixture of olive oil, ginger, fish sauce, 4 cloves of garlic, soy sauce, and sesame oil into a plastic bag containing beef sirloin tips and shake it well to get beef coated with the mixture.
- Refrigerate it for at least two straight hours before removing the beef from the marinade.
- Cook this beef in hot oil for about seven minutes or until you see that it is no longer pink before setting it aside on a plate.
- Turn down the heat to medium and cook garlic, onion and green onion for about five minutes before adding green beans, lime juice, basil, mint, beef broth, red

pepper flakes, pepper and also the beef.

- Mix it thoroughly before adding cilantro.

Serving: 5

Timing Information:

Preparation	Cooking	Total Time
20 mins	30 mins	2 hr 50 mins

Nutritional Information:

Calories	475 kcal
Carbohydrates	8.8 g
Cholesterol	101 mg
Fat	34.4 g
Fiber	2 g
Protein	31.7 g
Sodium	1174 mg

* Percent Daily Values are based on a 2,000 calorie diet.

Shrimp Soup

Ingredients

- 1 tbsp vegetable oil
- 2 tsps minced fresh garlic
- 2 tsps minced fresh ginger root
- 1 (10 ounce) package frozen chopped spinach, thawed and drained
- salt and black pepper to taste
- 2 quarts chicken stock
- 1 cup shrimp stock
- 1 tsp hot pepper sauce(optional)
- 1 tsp hoisin sauce(optional)
- 20 peeled and deveined medium shrimp
- 1 (6.75 ounce) package long rice noodles (rice vermicelli)
- 2 green onions, chopped(optional)

Directions

- Cook garlic and ginger for about one minute before adding spinach, pepper and salt, and cooking it for 3 more minutes to get the spinach tender.
- Add chicken stock, hoisin sauce, shrimp stock and hot pepper sauce, and cook this for a few more minutes.
- In the end, add noodles and shrimp into it, and cook it for 4 minutes before adding green onions cooking it for another five minutes.
- Add salt and pepper according to your taste before serving.
- Enjoy.

Serving: 6

Timing Information:

Preparation	Cooking	Total Time
15 mins	20 mins	40 mins

Nutritional Information:

Calories	212 kcal
Carbohydrates	28.6 g
Cholesterol	52 mg
Fat	4.7 g
Fiber	2.7 g
Protein	14.4 g
Sodium	1156 mg

* Percent Daily Values are based on a 2,000 calorie diet.

CHINESE PORK CHOPS

Ingredients

- 2 tbsps brown sugar
- 2 tbsps honey
- 2 tbsps fish sauce
- 3 tbsps vegetable oil
- 2 tbsps soy sauce
- 1/2 tsp Worcestershire sauce
- 1/2 tsp minced fresh ginger root
- 1 tsp Chinese five-spice powder
- 1 tsp sesame oil
- 1 tsp minced shallot
- 6 cloves garlic, minced
- 1/2 onion, chopped
- 2 lemon grass, chopped
- 1/4 tsp salt
- 1/2 tsp ground black pepper
- 6 thin, boneless center-cut pork chops
- 1/4 cup vegetable oil

Directions

- Add the mixture brown sugar, honey, lemon grass, soy sauce, Worcestershire sauce, ginger, five-spice powder, sesame oil, fish sauce, shallot, garlic, onion, vegetable oil, salt, and pepper into a plastic bag containing pork chops, and mix it well to coat pork chops thoroughly before refrigerating it for at least eight hours.
- Cook these pork chops on a preheated grill that is lightly oiled for about four minutes each side.
- Serve.

Serving: 6

Timing Information:

Preparation	Cooking	Total Time
15 mins	10 mins	8 hr 25 mins

Nutritional Information:

Calories	416 kcal
Carbohydrates	15 g
Cholesterol	63 mg
Fat	28.8 g
Fiber	0.3 g
Protein	24.5 g
Sodium	814 mg

* Percent Daily Values are based on a 2,000 calorie diet.

Tofu Based Salad In Vietnam

Ingredients

- 1 tbsp vegetable oil
- 2 tbsps chopped garlic
- 1 (14 ounce) package tofu, drained and cubed
- 1/2 cup peanuts
- 2 tbsps soy sauce
- 2 large cucumbers, peeled and thinly sliced
- 1/2 cup Vietnamese sweet chili sauce
- 1/4 cup lime juice
- 1 bunch chopped cilantro leaves

Directions

- Cook garlic in hot oil for about thirty seconds before adding tofu and peanuts, and cooking it again until tofu is lightly brown.

- Now add soy sauce and cook until you see that it is completely absorbed before refrigerating it for at least one hour.
- In the mixture of chili sauce, cilantro, sliced cucumbers and lime juice add tofu, and mix it thoroughly before serving.
- Enjoy.

Serving: 6

Timing Information:

Preparation	Cooking	Total Time
15 mins	25 mins	1 hr 40 mins

Nutritional Information:

Calories	200 kcal
Carbohydrates	18.4 g
Cholesterol	0 mg
Fat	11.7 g
Fiber	2.6 g
Protein	9.5 g
Sodium	636 mg

* Percent Daily Values are based on a 2,000 calorie diet.

BEEF AND LETTUCE

Ingredients

- 1 cup uncooked long grain white rice
- 2 cups water
- 5 tsps white sugar
- 1 clove garlic, minced
- 1/4 cup fish sauce
- 5 tbsps water
- 1 1/2 tbsps chili sauce
- 1 lemon, juiced
- 2 tbsps vegetable oil
- 3 cloves garlic, minced
- 1 pound ground beef
- 1 tbsp ground cumin
- 1 (28 ounce) can canned diced tomatoes
- 2 cups lettuce leaves, torn into 1/2 inch wide strips

Directions

- Bring the water containing rice to boil before turning down the heat to low and cooking for 25 minutes.
- Add mashed sugar and garlic to the mixture of chili sauce, fish sauce, lemon juice and water in a medium sized bowl.
- Cook garlic in hot oil before adding beef and cumin, and cooking all this until you see that it is brown.
- Now add half of that fish sauce mixture and tomatoes into the pan, and after turning down the heat to low, cook all this for twenty more minutes.
- Add lettuce into this beef mixture before serving this over the cooked rice along with that remaining fish sauce.

Serving: 6

Timing Information:

Preparation	Cooking	Total Time
15 mins	45 mins	1 hr

Nutritional Information:

Calories	529 kcal
Carbohydrates	56.9 g
Cholesterol	69 mg
Fat	21 g
Fiber	4 g
Protein	26.3 g
Sodium	1481 mg

* Percent Daily Values are based on a 2,000 calorie diet.

Rice-Noodle Salad

Ingredients

- 5 cloves garlic
- 1 cup loosely packed chopped cilantro
- 1/2 jalapeno pepper, seeded and minced
- 3 tbsps white sugar
- 1/4 cup fresh lime juice
- 3 tbsps vegetarian fish sauce
- 1 (12 ounce) package dried rice noodles
- 2 carrots, julienned
- 1 cucumber, halved lengthwise and chopped
- 1/4 cup chopped fresh mint
- 4 leaves napa cabbage
- 1/4 cup unsalted peanuts
- 4 sprigs fresh mint

Directions

- Add a mashed mixture of hot pepper, garlic and cilantro into the bowl containing mixture of lime juice, sugar and fish sauce before letting it stand for at least five minutes.
- Cook rice noodles in boiling salty water for two minutes before draining it and passing it through cold water to stop the process of cooking.
- Mix sauce, carrots, cucumber, noodles, mint and Napa in large sized serving bowl very thoroughly before garnishing it with peanuts and mint sprigs.

Serving: 4

Timing Information:

Preparation	Cooking	Total Time
15 mins		15 mins

Nutritional Information:

Calories	432 kcal
Carbohydrates	89.5 g
Cholesterol	0 mg
Fat	5.3 g
Fiber	4.1 g
Protein	6.6 g
Sodium	188 mg

* Percent Daily Values are based on a 2,000 calorie diet.

CHICKEN WINGS IN VIETNAM

Ingredients

- 12 chicken wings, tips removed and wings cut in half at joint
- 2 cloves garlic, peeled and coarsely chopped
- 1/2 onion, cut into chunks
- 1/4 cup soy sauce
- 1/4 cup Asian fish sauce
- 2 tbsps fresh lemon juice
- 2 tbsps sesame oil
- 1 tsp salt
- 1 tsp freshly ground black pepper
- 1 tbsp garlic powder
- 1 tbsp white sugar

Directions

- Into the mixture of chicken wings, onion and garlic in large sized bowl; add fish sauce, sesame oi, salt, sugar, garlic powder, pepper and lemon juice before refrigerating it covered for at least two hours.

- Preheat your oven at 400 degrees F and place aluminum foil in the baking dish.
- Reserving some marinade for brushing; place all the wings on the baking dish and bake it for about 30 minutes or until you see that these have turned golden brown.

Serving: 4

Timing Information:

Preparation	Cooking	Total Time
15 mins	30 mins	2 hr 45 mins

Nutritional Information:

Calories	716 kcal
Carbohydrates	9.1 g
Cholesterol	213 mg
Fat	50.9 g
Fiber	0.8 g
Protein	53 g
Sodium	2781 mg

* Percent Daily Values are based on a 2,000 calorie diet.

Beef Pho

Ingredients

- 4 quarts beef broth
- 1 large onion, sliced into rings
- 6 slices fresh ginger root
- 1 lemon grass
- 1 cinnamon stick
- 1 tsp whole black peppercorns
- 1 pound sirloin tip, cut into thin slices
- 1/2 pound bean sprouts
- 1 cup fresh basil leaves
- 1 cup fresh mint leaves
- 1 cup loosely packed cilantro leaves
- 3 fresh jalapeno peppers, sliced into rings
- 2 limes, cut into wedges
- 2 (8 ounce) packages dried rice noodles
- 1/2 tbsp hoisin sauce
- 1 dash hot pepper sauce
- 3 tbsps fish sauce

Directions

- Bring the mixture of broth, onion, lemon grass, cinnamon, ginger and peppercorns to boil before turning down the heat to low and cooking it for about one hour.
- Place bean sprouts, basil, cilantro, chilies, mint and lime on a platter very neatly.
- Place noodles in hot water for about 15 minutes before placing it in six different bowls evenly.
- Put raw beef over it before pouring in hot broth.
- Serve it with the platter and sauces.

Serving: 6

Timing Information:

Preparation	Cooking	Total Time
10 mins	1 hr 20 mins	1 hr 30 mins

Nutritional Information:

Calories	528 kcal
Carbohydrates	73.1 g
Cholesterol	51 mg
Fat	13.6 g
Fiber	3.9 g
Protein	27.1 g
Sodium	2844 mg

* Percent Daily Values are based on a 2,000 calorie diet.

A CHICKEN & CURRY SOUP FROM SOUTHEAST ASIA

Ingredients

- 2 tbsps vegetable oil
- 1 (3 pound) whole chicken, skin removed and cut into pieces
- 1 onion, cut into chunks
- 2 shallots, thinly sliced
- 2 cloves garlic, chopped
- 1/8 cup thinly sliced fresh ginger root
- 1 stalk lemon grass, cut into 2 inch pieces
- 4 tbsps curry powder
- 1 green bell pepper, cut into 1 inch pieces
- 2 carrots, sliced diagonally
- 1 quart chicken broth
- 1 quart water
- 2 tbsps fish sauce
- 2 kaffir lime leaves
- 1 bay leaf

- 2 tsps red pepper flakes
- 8 small potatoes, quartered
- 1 (14 ounce) can coconut milk
- 1 bunch fresh cilantro

Directions

- Cook onion and chicken in hot oil until you see that onions are soft and then set it aside for later use.
- Cook shallots in the same pan for one minute before adding garlic, lemon grass, ginger and curry powder, and cooking it for another five minutes.
- Add pepper and carrots before stirring in chicken, onion, fish sauce, chicken broth and water.
- Also add lime leaves, red pepper flakes and bay leaf before bringing all this to boil and adding potatoes.
- Add coconut milk and cook it for 60 minutes after turning down the heat to low.

- Garnish with a sprig of fresh cilantro.
- Serve.

Serving: 8

Timing Information:

Preparation	Cooking	Total Time
30 mins	2 hr	2 hr 30 mins

Nutritional Information:

Calories	512 kcal
Carbohydrates	40.6 g
Cholesterol	75 mg
Fat	26.8 g
Fiber	6.7 g
Protein	29.8 g
Sodium	374 mg

* Percent Daily Values are based on a 2,000 calorie diet.

A Vietnamese Condiment

Ingredients

- 1/4 cup white sugar
- 1/2 cup warm water
- 1/4 cup fish sauce
- 1/3 cup distilled white vinegar
- 1/2 lemon, juiced
- 3 cloves garlic, minced
- 3 Thai chile peppers, chopped
- 1 green onion, thinly sliced

Directions

- In a mixture of warm water and sugar; add fish sauce, garlic, green onion, lemon juice, vinegar and chili pepper.
- Mix all this very thoroughly before serving.
- Enjoy.

NOTE: Use this condiment for dipping spring rolls in, or as a topping for jasmine rice.

Serving: 5

Timing Information:

Preparation	Cooking	Total Time
15 mins		15 mins

Nutritional Information:

Calories	15 kcal
Carbohydrates	3.7 g
Cholesterol	0 mg
Fat	0 g
Fiber	0.3 g
Protein	0.4 g
Sodium	220 mg

* Percent Daily Values are based on a 2,000 calorie diet.

La Sa Ga

(A Vietnamese Soup)

Ingredients

- 3 tbsps peanut oil
- 1 cup diced onion
- 3 tbsps minced garlic
- 1 cup coconut milk, divided
- 1 tbsp red curry paste, or more to taste
- 2 cooked chicken breast halves, shredded
- 8 cups chicken stock
- 6 tbsps soy sauce, or to taste
- 1/4 cup fish sauce, or to taste
- 1 1/2 pounds angel hair pasta
- 1/4 cup chopped fresh basil, or to taste

Directions

- Cook onion and garlic in hot oil for about four minutes before adding coconut milk and stirring it continuously for about two minutes.
- Now add curry paste and stir it well for about two more minutes.
- Introduce chicken stock into the pan and cook it for about four minutes after turning up the heat to medium.
- Cook it for another four minutes after adding the remaining coconut milk.
- Stir in angel hair pasta before covering up the pot and cooking it for ten more minutes.
- Add basil before serving.

Serving: 8

Timing Information:

Preparation	Cooking	Total Time
20 mins	20 mins	40 mins

Nutritional Information:

Calories	333 kcal
Carbohydrates	41.8 g
Cholesterol	15 mg
Fat	13.5 g
Fiber	3.1 g
Protein	15.1 g
Sodium	1710 mg

* Percent Daily Values are based on a 2,000 calorie diet.

LEMON GRASS CHICKEN

Ingredients

- 2 tbsps vegetable oil
- 1 lemon grass, minced
- 1 (3 pound) whole chicken, cut into pieces
- 2/3 cup water
- 1 tbsp fish sauce
- 1 1/2 tbsps curry powder
- 1 tbsp cornstarch
- 1 tbsp chopped cilantro(optional)

Directions

- Cook lemon grass in hot oil for about 5 minutes before adding chicken and cooking it until you see that the chicken is no longer pink from the center.
- Now add fish sauce, curry powder and water into the pan before

turning the heat up to high and cooking it for another 15 minutes.

- Now add the mixture of curry sauce and cornstarch into the pan, and cook all this for another five minutes.
- Garnish with cilantro before serving.

Serving: 4

Timing Information:

Preparation	Cooking	Total Time
15 mins	25 mins	40 mins

Nutritional Information:

Calories	813 kcal
Carbohydrates	4.6 g
Cholesterol	255 mg
Fat	58.4 g
Fiber	0.8 g
Protein	63.8 g
Sodium	515 mg

* Percent Daily Values are based on a 2,000 calorie diet.

A Sandwich In Vietnam

Ingredients

- 4 boneless pork loin chops, cut 1/4 inch thick
- 4 (7 inch) French bread baguettes, split lengthwise
- 4 tsps mayonnaise, or to taste
- 1 ounce chili sauce with garlic
- 1/4 cup fresh lime juice
- 1 small red onion, sliced into rings
- 1 medium cucumber, peeled and sliced lengthwise
- 2 tbsps chopped fresh cilantro
- salt and pepper to taste

Directions

- Put pork chops on the broiling pan and cook it for about 5 minutes or until you see that it is brown from each side.

- Put mayonnaise evenly on French rolls and also put one pork chop on each roll.
- Put chili sauce on the meat and add some lime juice, while topping it with onion, pepper, cucumber, salt and cilantro.
- Add some more lime juice just before serving.

Serving: 4

Timing Information:

Preparation	Cooking	Total Time
10 mins	5 mins	15 mins

Nutritional Information:

Calories	627 kcal
Carbohydrates	72.1 g
Cholesterol	124 mg
Fat	12.1 g
Fiber	3.3 g
Protein	55.3 g
Sodium	1005 mg

* Percent Daily Values are based on a 2,000 calorie diet.

Chapter 7: Ramen Noodles

Sesame Ramen Coleslaw

Ingredients

- 2 tbsps vegetable oil
- 3 tbsps white wine vinegar
- 2 tbsps white sugar
- 1 (3 ounce) package chicken flavored ramen noodles, crushed, seasoning packet reserved
- 1/2 tsp salt
- 1/2 tsp ground black pepper
- 2 tbsps sesame seeds
- 1/4 cup sliced almonds
- 1/2 medium head cabbage, shredded
- 5 green onions, chopped

Directions

- Set your oven at 350 degrees F and also put some oil on the baking dish.
- Mix oil, ramen noodle mix, salt, vinegar, pepper and sugar in a bowl to be used as a dressing.
- Bake sesame seeds and almonds in the preheated oven for about 10 minutes.
- Coat the mixture of cabbage, crushed ramen noodles and greens onions with the dressing very thoroughly before topping it with sesame seeds and almonds.
- Serve.

Serving: 4

Timing Information:

Preparation	Cooking	Total Time
15 mins	10 mins	25 mins

Nutritional Information:

Calories	253 kcal
Carbohydrates	30.5 g
Cholesterol	0 mg
Fat	12.5 g
Fiber	5.1 g
Protein	7.1 g
Sodium	543 mg

* Percent Daily Values are based on a 2,000 calorie diet.

BROCCOLI RAMEN SALAD

Ingredients

- 1 (16 ounce) package broccoli coleslaw mix
- 2 (3 ounce) packages chicken flavored ramen noodles
- 1 bunch green onions, chopped
- 1 cup unsalted peanuts
- 1 cup sunflower seeds
- 1/2 cup white sugar
- 1/4 cup vegetable oil
- 1/3 cup cider vinegar

Directions

- Coat a mixture of green onions, slaw and broken noodles with the mixture of sugar, ramen seasoning packets, oil and vinegar very thoroughly before refrigerating it for at least one hour.
- Garnish with peanuts and sunflower seeds before serving it.

Serving: 6

Timing Information:

Preparation	Cooking	Total Time
15 mins		45 mins

Nutritional Information:

Calories	280 kcal
Carbohydrates	53.6 g
Cholesterol	0 mg
Fat	4.4 g
Fiber	1.3 g
Protein	10.4 g
Sodium	1351 mg

* Percent Daily Values are based on a 2,000 calorie diet.

VENETIAN BEEF RAMEN STIR-FRY

Ingredients

- 1 pound ground beef, or to taste
- 16 slices pepperoni, or to taste
- 1 (14.5 ounce) can diced tomatoes
- 1 cup water
- 2 (3 ounce) packages beef-flavored ramen noodles
- 1 green bell peppers, cut into strips
- 1 cup shredded mozzarella cheese

Directions

- Cook beef and pepperoni slices over high heat in a large skillet for about 7 minutes before adding tomatoes, content of seasoning packet content from ramen noodles and water into skillet containing beef.
- After breaking ramen noodles into half, add this to the beef mixture along with green bell pepper and cook all this for about

five minutes or until you see that noodles are soft.

- Turn the heat off before adding mozzarella cheese and letting it melt down before serving.

Serving: 6

Timing Information:

Preparation	Cooking	Total Time
10 mins	15 mins	45 mins

Nutritional Information:

Calories	297 kcal
Carbohydrates	7.4 g
Cholesterol	78 mg
Fat	18.4 g
Fiber	1.2 g
Protein	23.6 g
Sodium	546 mg

* Percent Daily Values are based on a 2,000 calorie diet.

NATURAL RAMEN NOODLES

Ingredients

- 4 cups vegetable broth
- 4 cups water
- 1 tbsp soy sauce
- 1 tbsp sesame oil
- 1 tbsp ground ginger
- 1 tbsp Sriracha hot sauce
- 9 ounces soba noodles

Directions

- Bring everything except noodles to boil before adding noodles and cooking it for about seven minutes or until you see that they are tender.
- Take noodles out into bowls and top with broth according to your choice.

Serving: 4

Timing Information:

Preparation	Cooking	Total Time
10 mins	10 mins	20 mins

Nutritional Information:

Calories	280 kcal
Carbohydrates	53.6 g
Cholesterol	0 mg
Fat	4.4 g
Fiber	1.3 g
Protein	10.4 g
Sodium	1351 mg

* Percent Daily Values are based on a 2,000 calorie diet.

CABBAGE RAMEN SALAD I

Ingredients

- 1/2 large head cabbage, coarsely chopped
- 1 (3 ounce) package ramen noodles, crushed
- 1/2 cup sunflower seeds
- 1/2 cup vegetable oil
- 3 tbsps white sugar
- 3 tbsps distilled white vinegar

Directions

- Pour a mixture of vinegar, ramen flavor packet, sugar and oil over the mixture of cabbage, sunflower seeds and noodles.
- Mix it very thoroughly before serving.

Serving: 6

Timing Information:

Preparation	Cooking	Total Time
15 mins	10 mins	25 mins

Nutritional Information:

Calories	266 kcal
Carbohydrates	16.2 g
Cholesterol	< 1 mg
Fat	22.6 g
Fiber	3.2 g
Protein	1.8 g
Sodium	82 mg

* Percent Daily Values are based on a 2,000 calorie diet.

RAMEN FOR COLLEGE

Ingredients

- 2 1/2 cups water
- 1 carrot, sliced
- 4 fresh mushrooms, sliced
- 1 (3 ounce) package ramen noodle pasta with flavor packet
- 1 egg, lightly beaten
- 1/4 cup milk (optional)

Directions

- Cook carrots and mushrooms in boiling water for about seven minutes before adding noodles and flavoring packets, and cooking all this for three more minutes.
- Pour egg into the mixture very slowly, while stirring continuously for thirty seconds to get the egg cooked.
- Add some milk before serving.

Serving: 1

Timing Information:

Preparation	Cooking	Total Time
5 mins	10 mins	15 mins

Nutritional Information:

Calories	500 kcal
Carbohydrates	66 g
Cholesterol	191 mg
Fat	19.2 g
Fiber	4.5 g
Protein	17.4 g
Sodium	1796 mg

* Percent Daily Values are based on a 2,000 calorie diet.

EASY RAMEN SOUP

Ingredients

- 3 1/2 cups vegetable broth
- 1 (3.5 ounce) package ramen noodles with dried vegetables
- 2 tsps soy sauce
- 1/2 tsp chili oil
- 1/2 tsp minced fresh ginger root
- 2 green onions, sliced

Directions

- Bring a mixture of noodles and broth to boil over high heat before turning down the heat to medium and adding soy sauce, ginger and chili oil.
- Cook this for about 10 minutes before adding sesame oil.
- Garnish this with green onions before serving.

Serving: 2

Timing Information:

Preparation	Cooking	Total Time
5 mins	10 mins	15 mins

Nutritional Information:

Calories	291 kcal
Carbohydrates	42.4 g
Cholesterol	0 mg
Fat	10.2 g
Fiber	2.2 g
Protein	6.9 g
Sodium	1675 mg

* Percent Daily Values are based on a 2,000 calorie diet.

CHEESY RAMEN

Ingredients

- 2 cups water
- 1 (3 ounce) package any flavor ramen noodles
- 1 slice American cheese

Directions

- Cook ramen noodles in boiling water for about 2 minutes and drain it with the help of colander before stirring in seasoning packet and cheese.
- Serve.

Serving: 1

Timing Information:

Preparation	Cooking	Total Time
5 mins		5 mins

Nutritional Information:

Calories	163 kcal
Carbohydrates	7.9 g
Cholesterol	27 mg
Fat	11.3 g
Fiber	0.4 g
Protein	7.5 g
Sodium	733 mg

* Percent Daily Values are based on a 2,000 calorie diet.

CABBAGE RAMEN SALAD II

Ingredients

- 1 1/4 pounds red cabbage, chopped
- 2 (3 ounce) packages ramen noodles, broken into small pieces
- 1 cup chopped red bell pepper
- 1 cup chopped green onion
- 3/4 cup slivered almonds
- 1/2 cup roasted sunflower seeds
- 1/2 cup toasted sesame seeds
- 1/2 cup white sugar
- 1/2 cup peanut oil
- 1/2 cup olive oil
- 1/4 cup red wine vinegar
- 1/2 tsp ground black pepper

Directions

- Combine all the ingredients mentioned above very thoroughly in a large re-sealable bag very thoroughly before serving it to anyone.

Serving: 12

Timing Information:

Preparation	Cooking	Total Time
30 mins		30 mins

Nutritional Information:

Calories	384 kcal
Carbohydrates	26.6 g
Cholesterol	0 mg
Fat	29.7 g
Fiber	3.7 g
Protein	5.7 g
Sodium	290 mg

* Percent Daily Values are based on a 2,000 calorie diet.

Ramen Frittata

Ingredients

- 2 (3 ounce) packages chicken flavored ramen noodles
- 6 eggs
- 2 tsps butter
- 1/2 cup shredded Cheddar cheese

Directions

- Cook ramen noodles in boiling water for about 2 minutes and drain it with the help of colander.
- Pour the mixture of eggs and content of seasoning packets over noodles before cooking this in hot butter for about seven minutes.
- Turn it over after cutting it into four slices and brown both sides.
- Put some cheese over the top before serving.

Serving: 4

Timing Information:

Preparation	Cooking	Total Time
5 mins	15 mins	20 mins

Nutritional Information:

Calories	339 kcal
Carbohydrates	28.8 g
Cholesterol	302 mg
Fat	15.7 g
Fiber	1.2 g
Protein	20.3 g
Sodium	681 mg

* Percent Daily Values are based on a 2,000 calorie diet.

SPINACH RAMEN PASTA SALAD

Ingredients

- 2 (3 ounce) packages chicken flavored ramen noodles
- 8 cups torn spinach leaves
- 2 cups cooked and cubed chicken
- 1 cup seedless red grapes, halved
- 1 cup sliced red bell peppers
- 1/2 cup chopped cashews
- 1/2 cup Gorgonzola cheese, crumbled
- 4 cloves garlic, minced
- 1 lemon, juiced
- 1/3 cup olive oil
- 1/4 cup light mayonnaise
- 1 red bell pepper, sliced
- 20 grape clusters, for garnish

Directions

- Cook ramen noodles in boiling water for about 2 minutes and drain it with the help of colander.
- Mix torn spinach leaves, halved grapes, blue cheese, cooked turkey or chicken, red pepper,

531

cashews and ramen noodles very thorough in a large bowl.

- In another bowl; whisk lemon juice, flavor packets, oil, garlic and mayonnaise very thoroughly.
- Pour this dressing that you just prepared over the salad and garnish this salad with some red pepper rings and small grape clusters.
- Serve.

Serving: 2

Timing Information:

Preparation	Cooking	Total Time
15 mins	10 mins	25 mins

Nutritional Information:

Calories	147 kcal
Carbohydrates	11 g
Cholesterol	17 mg
Fat	8.6 g
Fiber	1.3 g
Protein	7.2 g
Sodium	177 mg

* Percent Daily Values are based on a 2,000 calorie diet.

Chicken Ramen Stir-Fry

Ingredients

- 1 1/2 cups hot water
- 1 (3 ounce) package Oriental-flavor ramen noodle soup mix
- 2 tsps vegetable oil, divided
- 8 ounces skinless, boneless chicken breast halves, cut into 2-inch strips
- 2 cups broccoli florets
- 1 cup sliced onion wedges
- 2 cloves garlic, minced
- 1 cup fresh bean sprouts
- 1/2 cup water
- 1/2 cup sliced water chestnuts
- 1 tsp soy sauce
- 1 tsp oyster sauce
- 1/4 tsp chili-garlic sauce (such as Sriracha®), or to taste
- 1 roma tomato, cut into wedges

Directions

- Cook ramen noodles in boiling water for about 2 minutes and drain it with the help of colander.

- Now cook chicken in hot oil for about 5 minutes and set it aside in a bowl.
- In the same skillet; Cook broccoli, garlic and onion for about three minutes before adding noodles, water, oyster sauce, chili garlic sauce, water chestnuts, bean sprouts, soy sauce and seasoning from the ramen noodle package.
- Cook all this for about 5 minutes before adding tomato wedges and cooking it for three more minutes.

Serving: 2

Timing Information:

Preparation	Cooking	Total Time
15 mins	15 mins	30 mins

Nutritional Information:

Calories	438 kcal
Carbohydrates	47.6 g
Cholesterol	65 mg
Fat	14.1 g
Fiber	6.4 g
Protein	31.9 g
Sodium	1118 mg

* Percent Daily Values are based on a 2,000 calorie diet.

PEANUT PASTA RAMEN NOODLES

Ingredients

- 1/3 cup peanut butter
- 3 tbsps vegetable oil
- 3 tbsps vinegar
- 2 tbsps soy sauce
- 1 clove garlic, minced
- 1 tsp white sugar
- 1/4 tsp cayenne pepper, or to taste
- 4 (3 ounce) packages ramen noodle soup (seasoning packets reserved for another use)
- 1/2 small cucumber, peeled and cut into matchsticks
- 1 green onion, thinly sliced
- 1/4 cup chopped cilantro
- 2 tbsps chopped salted peanuts

Directions

- Cook ramen noodles in boiling water for about 2 minutes and drain it with the help of colander

- Pour the mixture of peanut butter, vegetable oil, garlic, vinegar, soy sauce, sugar, and cayenne over noodles in a bowl, and mix it very thoroughly.
- Add cucumber and green onion into it.
- Garnish all this with peanuts and cilantro before serving.

Serving: 4

Timing Information:

Preparation	Cooking	Total Time
15 mins	5 mins	20 mins

Nutritional Information:

Calories	613 kcal
Carbohydrates	62.5 g
Cholesterol	0 mg
Fat	35.9 g
Fiber	4.2 g
Protein	13.5 g
Sodium	2224 mg

* Percent Daily Values are based on a 2,000 calorie diet.

CHESTNUT & PEPPERS RAMEN SALAD

Ingredients

- 4 (3 ounce) packages chicken flavored ramen noodles
- 1 cup diced celery
- 1 (8 ounce) can water chestnuts, drained and sliced
- 1/2 red onion, diced
- 1/2 green bell pepper, diced
- 4 ounces frozen green peas
- 1 cup mayonnaise

Directions

- Cook noodles according to the direction of the packets and drain it with the help of colander.
- Pour mixture of mayonnaise and ramen noodle seasoning mix over the mixture of noodles, peas, celery, bell pepper, water chestnuts and red onion before refrigerating for at least an hour.
- Serve.

Serving: 12

Timing Information:

Preparation	Cooking	Total Time
15 mins	10 mins	25 mins

Nutritional Information:

Calories	249 kcal
Carbohydrates	23.7 g
Cholesterol	7 mg
Fat	15 g
Fiber	2 g
Protein	5.3 g
Sodium	427 mg

* Percent Daily Values are based on a 2,000 calorie diet.

Slow Cooker Thai Ramen

Ingredients

- 3 cups water
- 1 tbsp soy sauce
- 1 (13.5 ounce) can light coconut milk
- 1 tbsp Thai garlic chile paste
- 1/2 cup peanut butter
- 1 onion, chopped
- 2 cloves garlic, minced
- 1 inch piece fresh ginger, grated
- 2 green bell peppers, diced
- 2 pounds skinless, boneless chicken thighs, diced
- 2 (3 ounce) packages ramen noodles
- 1/2 cup diced cucumber
- 2 green onions, chopped
- 1/2 cup chopped fresh cilantro
- 1/2 cup chopped fresh basil

Directions

- Cook the mixture of peanut butter onion, garlic, water, soy

sauce, ginger, green coconut milk, chili paste, pepper and diced chicken over high heat for about four hours before adding ramen noodles.
- Cook all this on high heat for another 20 minutes to get the noodles soft before adding ramen seasoning packets.
- Garnish all this with cucumbers, basil, green onions and cilantro.
- Serve.

Serving: 6

Timing Information:

Preparation	Cooking	Total Time
20 mins	4 hr 15 mins	4 hr 35 mins

Nutritional Information:

Calories	479 kcal
Carbohydrates	16.3 g
Cholesterol	85 mg
Fat	32.5 g
Fiber	3.2 g
Protein	31.3 g
Sodium	458 mg

* Percent Daily Values are based on a 2,000 calorie diet.

Nutty Ramen Salad

Ingredients

- 1 (16 ounce) package coleslaw mix
- 8 green onions, chopped
- 1/2 cup butter or margarine
- 1 head fresh broccoli, cut into florets
- 2 (3 ounce) packages chicken flavored ramen noodles
- 1 cup slivered almonds
- 1 cup unsalted sunflower seeds
- 1/2 cup white sugar
- 1/4 cup apple cider vinegar
- 1/2 cup vegetable oil
- 1 tsp soy sauce

Directions

- Mix broccoli, coleslaw mix and green onion in a bowl and set it aside.
- Cook the mixture of ramen noodles, sunflower seeds, seasoning packets and almonds in hot butter for about eight

minutes or until the nuts are toasted.

- Pour the mixture of sugar, soy sauce and oil over the mixture of noodles mixture and slaw mixture.
- Mix it very thoroughly before serving.

Serving: 12

Timing Information:

Preparation	Cooking	Total Time
20 mins	15 mins	35 mins

Nutritional Information:

Calories	395 kcal
Carbohydrates	28.9 g
Cholesterol	23 mg
Fat	28.8 g
Fiber	3.7 g
Protein	8 g
Sodium	252 mg

* Percent Daily Values are based on a 2,000 calorie diet.

Tofu Ramen Lo-Mein

Ingredients

- 1 (16 ounce) package extra firm tofu
- 2 tbsps olive oil
- 2 (3 ounce) packages Oriental flavored ramen noodles
- 1 (16 ounce) package frozen stir-fry vegetables
- 1 1/2 cups water
- 1 tbsp soy sauce, or to taste

Directions

- Dry out tofu and cut into small pieces.
- Cook tofu in hot olive oil for about 15 minutes.
- Cook ramen noodles in boiling water for about 2 minutes and drain it with the help of colander
- Cook the mixture of tofu, stir-fry vegetables and ramen noodle seasoning packet for a few minutes or until the vegetables are tender.

- Add noodles and mix it well before seasoning it with soy sauce.
- Serve.

Serving: 4

Timing Information:

Preparation	Cooking	Total Time
5 mins	25 mins	30 mins

Nutritional Information:

Calories	383 kcal
Carbohydrates	38.6 g
Cholesterol	< 1 mg
Fat	19.8 g
Fiber	3.9 g
Protein	17.1 g
Sodium	1333 mg

* Percent Daily Values are based on a 2,000 calorie diet.

MAGGIE'S FAVORITE RAMEN SALAD

Ingredients

Salad:

- 2 (3 ounce) packages chicken-flavored ramen noodles, broken into pieces, seasoning packets reserved
- 1/2 cup raw sunflower seeds
- 1/2 cup slivered almonds
- 1 (16 ounce) package coleslaw mix
- 3 green onions, chopped
- Dressing:
- 1/2 cup olive oil
- 3 tbsps white vinegar
- 1 tbsp white sugar
- 1/2 tsp ground black pepper

Directions

- Set your oven at 350 degrees F.
- Bake noodles, almonds and sunflower seeds in the preheated oven for about 15 minutes before adding this on top of the mixture

of green onions and coleslaw mix in a bowl.

- Now pour the mixture of olive oil, vinegar, reserved ramen seasoning packets, sugar, and black pepper over coleslaw mixture.
- Serve.

Serving: 6

Timing Information:

Preparation	Cooking	Total Time
15 mins	10 mins	55 mins

Nutritional Information:

Calories	450 kcal
Carbohydrates	34.9 g
Cholesterol	6 mg
Fat	31.1 g
Fiber	4 g
Protein	9.9 g
Sodium	324 mg

* Percent Daily Values are based on a 2,000 calorie diet.

GROUND BEEF RAMEN

Ingredients

- 1 pound ground beef
- 1 (3 ounce) package Oriental flavored ramen noodles
- 1 (14.5 ounce) can diced tomatoes
- 1 (10 ounce) can whole kernel corn

Directions

- Cook ground beef over high heat in a skillet until no longer pink before adding noodles, corn and tomatoes.
- Bring all this to boil before turning down the heat to low and cooking it for another 10 minutes.
- Stir continuously in all this time.
- Serve.

Serving: 4

Timing Information:

Preparation	Cooking	Total Time
10 mins	10 mins	20 mins

Nutritional Information:

Calories	368 kcal
Carbohydrates	30.2 g
Cholesterol	69 mg
Fat	17.1 g
Fiber	2.7 g
Protein	23.3 g
Sodium	843 mg

* Percent Daily Values are based on a 2,000 calorie diet.

Broccoli Almond Ramen Coleslaw

Ingredients

- 1 (12 ounce) package broccoli coleslaw mix
- 1/2 cup sunflower seeds
- 1/2 cup slivered almonds
- 1 (3 ounce) package Oriental-flavored ramen noodles, broken into small pieces
- 1/2 cup canola oil
- 1/4 cup white sugar
- 1/4 cup white wine vinegar
- 4 green onions, chopped

Directions

- Pour a mixture of canola oil, ramen noodle seasoning packet, sugar and vinegar over the mixture of broccoli coleslaw mix, sunflower seeds, almonds, and ramen noodles before adding green onions into it and refrigerating all this for 90 minutes.

- Serve.

Serving: 8

Timing Information:

Preparation	Cooking	Total Time
15 mins		1 hr 35 mins

Nutritional Information:

Calories	301 kcal
Carbohydrates	19 g
Cholesterol	0 mg
Fat	23.8 g
Fiber	3 g
Protein	4.6 g
Sodium	233 mg

* Percent Daily Values are based on a 2,000 calorie diet.

Chapter 8: Specialty Asian Bento (Japanese Lunch) Dim Sum (Asian Dumplings)

Egg Salad Sandwich Bento

Ingredients

- 2 slices, bread of your choice
- 1 hard boiled egg, peeled
- 1 Tbsp. Japanese mayonnaise
- Salt
- Freshly ground black pepper
- pinch of sugar (optional)*

Directions

- Take out a boiled egg and mash it in a small bowl before adding mayonnaise and mixing it well.

- Now add some salt and pepper into it according to your taste and mix more.
- Now place this egg mixture between the slices of bread.
- Cut sandwiches in two or three parts according to the size of your box after cutting its edges.
- Put these sandwich slices in the box and in the remaining space, put some vegetables and fruits.

ASPARAGUS BEEF ROLL BENTO

Ingredients

- Onigiri (Rice Balls)
- Asparagus Beef Rolls
- Edamame
- Oranges
- Grapes
- Cherry tomatoes

Directions

- Make some Onigiri (Rice Balls) in a pan and let it cool down before using.
- Now take out asparagus beef rolls and heat them in a frying pan over medium heat until heated through and let it cool down as well.
- You need to cook edamame according to the instructions of the package and cool it down as well.
- Cut oranges and squeeze grape as well as tomatoes juice over it.

- When everything is cool enough, put them in the bento box.

TONKATSU BENTO

Ingredients

- Japanese rice
- Tonkatsu
- Tonkatsu sauce
- Tomatoes
- Lettuce
- Radish
- Pre-blanched broccoli
- Salad dressing of your choice

Directions

- Place cooked rice in half of the bento box and let it cool down.
- Now bake tonkatsu for about 2 minutes or until you see that it is warm enough.
- Place it on top of the rice and put some tonkatsu sauce over it.
- Dry every bit of water from tomatoes, radish and lettuce after washing them.
- Cut them into a reasonable size and place them in the box along with some broccoli.

- Put all the dressing in a sauce container and let everything in the box to cool down before closing.

HONEY SOY SAUCE CHICKEN BENTO

Ingredients

- Onigiri (Rice Balls) (Rice Ball)
- Honey Soy Sauce Chicken
- 1 egg + 1 tsp. sugar for Quick & Easy Tamagoyaki
- Shredded cabbage (with salt and pepper)
- Mini tomato
- Blueberries
- Plums
- Grapes

Directions

- Make some Onigiri (Rice Balls) in a pan and let it cool down before using it.
- Now cook tamagoyaki in a pan.
- Cook shredded cabbage in hot oil using the same frying pan as the rice and add some salt and pepper according to your taste before transferring all this to a silicon cup.

- Wash mini tomato as well as some fruits and cut them into appropriate size.
- Now place all this into the box.
- You need to make sure that everything is cool enough before you close the box.

SOBORO BENTO

Ingredients

- Japanese rice
- Soboro
- Lettuce for garnish
- Peaches
- Strawberries

Directions

- At first you need to place cooked Japanese rice in half of the bento box and let it cool down.
- Now heat up soboro in a pan until you see that it is thoroughly warmed.
- Place lettuce in the bento box after washing it.
- Now place green peas, ground chicken and egg on the rice very neatly.
- Also put some peaches and strawberries in the empty space of the box.

- You need to make sure that everything is cool enough before you close the box.

KARAAGE BENTO

Ingredients

- Karaage
- Onigiri (Rice Balls)
- Sauteed Spinach
- Pre-cooked Tamagoyaki (Japanese Rolled Omelette)
- Tomatoes
- Pre-blanched broccoli

Directions

- Firstly, take out karaage from your fridge and heat it up in a toaster oven until you see that it warm.
- In this time, cook Onigiri (Rice Balls) and place in the bento box very neatly.
- Cook spinach and corn in hot oil for a few minutes before putting them in the box.
- Now place the heated karaage in the box along with some washed tomatoes.

- Make some space for the thawed broccoli as well.
- Settle everything neatly in the bento box.
- You need to make sure that everything is cool before you close the box.

CUTE BENTO

Ingredients

For Characters

- 1 2"x2" cucumber peel
- 1 slice cheddar cheese
- 1 slice ham
- 1 small round carrot
- 1 sheet nori seaweed

For Sandwich

- 1 Tbsp. strawberry jam
- 1 slice cheddar cheese
- 1 slice cucumber
- 1 slice tomato
- 1 Tbsp. egg salad
- 1 Tbsp. Japanese mayonnaise

For Bento

- Lettuce
- Cherry tomatoes
- Fruits (oranges, strawberries, and Apple Bunny/Rabbit

- Veggies (cherry tomatoes and cucumbers)
- Octopus shape sausages

Directions

- You can make characters of your own choice beforehand.
- Now with the help of a cookie cutter, make a small sandwich from the large one.
- Now spread strawberry jam and egg salad on this bread.
- Also spread some mayonnaise before adding ham, cucumber, cheese and tomato with cucumber being on top.
- Now place these sandwiches and also the lettuce very neatly into the bento box.
- In the remaining space of bento box, place cherry tomatoes.

WINTER VEGETABLE BENTO

Ingredients

- 2 English cucumbers (the long kind that often comes shrink-wrapped in plastic), cut in half lengthwise, de-seeded and cut into chunks
- 2 medium carrots, peeled and sliced thinly (about 1/8" / 1/4 cm thickness)
- 3-4 cabbage leaves, roughly chopped (including the ribs, which can be thinly sliced and added)
- 1 small piece fresh ginger root, peeled and thinly sliced
- The peel of 1/4 yuzu fruit OR 2 teaspoons dried yuzu peel OR a piece of grapefruit peel plus a piece of lemon peel (unwaxed) without the white pith
- 1 teaspoon sea salt
- 2 teaspoons yuzu juice OR lemon juice
- 1 teaspoon soy sauce

- 1 teaspoon whole black peppercorns
- 1/2 teaspoon instant dashi stock granules (optional)

Directions

- Take all the ingredients mentioned above and put them in a sealable plastic bag.
- Mix them thoroughly, while massaging with your own hands for the perfect effect.
- Now place it in a refrigerator for the whole night and drain off every bit of liquid you can find after one night of refrigeration.
- Do add some extra seasoning if you think it needs more.
- Place in the bento box of your choice.

SWEET-SOUR RADISH PICKLES

Ingredients

- 1 cup rice vinegar
- 3/4 cup ume vinegar
- 1/4 cup strawberry syrup or honey

Directions

- Combine all the liquids thoroughly in a container.
- Now cut all the green leaves from the radishes and trim the hairy root.
- If you are using small radishes then leave them as is otherwise cut them into small pieces.
- Put these radishes into a containers that is non-reactive and pour pickling liquid into it before covering and refrigerating it for at least one day before you eat them
- You can use it with any bento that you have prepared.

VEGETABLE OR VEGETABLE-AND-CHICKEN MIX

Ingredients

- 4-5 dried shiitake mushrooms
- 1 medium carrot
- one 6-inch piece medium parsnip
- 1 aburaage (fried bean curd), or 120g / 4 oz boneless skinless chicken
- 400ml / 1 3/4 U.S. cups of the shiitake mushroom soaking liquid
- 1 tablespoon sake
- 1 tablespoon mirin (use 1/2 tablespoon sugar if you don't have this)
- 1 1/2 tablespoon light soy sauce
- 1/4 teaspoon salt

Directions

- At first you need to put mushroom soaking liquid, sake, salt, soy sauce and stock in a skillet, while mixing it well.

- Now add all the vegetables into it before bring it to boil at high heat.
- Now turn down the heat to low and cook for another 10 minutes.
- Put meat that you have decided to use for this recipe into the pan and cook for another 5 minutes to get it tendered.
- Now turn of the heat and let it cool down in the liquid.
- You can store this in a container by putting it in the refrigerator for a full week.
- Put this into the bento box.

Parsnip Kinpira

Ingredients

- 2 medium to large parsnips, scrubbed well and peeled (you can skip the peeling if the skin is not so tough and bumpy)
- 1/2 cup water
- 1 tablespoon light cooking oil such as light olive oil or canola oil
- 1 tablespoon toasted dark sesame oil
- 1 tablespoon sesame seeds
- 1/8 teaspoon (or to taste) dried red chili pepper flakes, or use ichimi togarashi instead
- 2 tablespoons soy sauce

Directions

- Take out parsnips and slice them into matchsticks shapes.
- Put these slices into boiling water and cook for about 3 minutes.
- Now cook them in hot oil for about 3 minutes before adding

sesame seeds, chili pepper and soy sauce.

- Kinpiras freezes very well, so you can freeze it and pack it in the bento box whenever you want.

CUCUMBER AND NASHI (ASIAN PEAR) SALAD

Ingredients

- 2 large cucumbers
- 1 medium to large Asian pear
- 1 teaspoon salt
- 1/2 tablespoon soy sauce
- 6 tablespoons rice vinegar
- 1 tablespoon sugar
- 1/3 teaspoon dried hot red chili pepper flakes

Directions

- Taking out all the seeds from cucumbers and cut cucumbers into small chunks.
- Now slice nashi pear after peeling very finely.
- Combine both in a bowl and then stir in some salt.
- Now pour into it the mixture of salt, sugar, soy sauce, chili pepper and vinegar.

- Mix it thoroughly before you put it in the refrigerator for a whole night.
- You can use it with almost every kind of bento.

JAPANESE BURGERS WITH BEAN SPROUTS

Ingredients

- 700g / about 1 1/2 lbs. ground beef or a 50/50 mix of ground pork and beef
- 1 medium onion, finely chopped
- 1/2 cup (120ml) panko or dried breadcrumbs
- 1-2 Tbsp. milk or water
- 1 egg
- 1 tsp. salt
- freshly ground black pepper
- 2 large handfuls of bean sprouts, with the 'bean' part removed, roughly chopped
- oil for cooking
- ketchup and/or Worcestershire sauce and/or 'Bulldog' sauce (optional)

Directions

- Cook onion in hot oil for about two minutes and in a bowl,

combine breadcrumbs, milk and water together.
- In a separate bowl; mix meat, pepper, egg, onion, salt, and breadcrumbs together very thoroughly.
- Now make some patties out of it.
- Now cook it over medium heat in hot oil for about 10 minutes each side.
- Add to bento box.
- Enjoy.

TACO MEAT MIX

Ingredients

- 1 kg (2 lb 2 oz) lean ground beef
- 1 red pepper
- 1 yellow pepper
- 1 medium carrot
- 1 medium onion
- 2 garlic cloves
- 3 Tbsp. tomato paste
- about 1/3 cup water (about 80ml)
- oil for cooking
- 1 Tbsp red chili powder, or more to taste
- 1 Tbsp sweet paprika powder
- 1 tsp. ground cumin
- 1 tsp. salt (or to taste)
- freshly ground black pepper

Directions

- Slice all the vegetables in this recipe very finely.
- Now cook all the vegetables in hot oil over medium heat in a frying pan for about 3 minutes before

you add ground beef and cook for another 5-8 minutes.

- Now add tomato sauce and water, and cook for another 3 minutes.
- Add all the spices and mix it well.
- Cook for another 5 minutes before you put it into the bento box.
- You can also keep them in the freezer for a whole month.

JAPANESE SHREDDED PICKLE-SALAD

Ingredients

- 1 teaspoon salt
- 2 cups finely shredded cabbage
- 1 cup finely shredded carrot
- 1 cup finely shredded cucumber
- 1/2 cup rice vinegar
- 4 tablespoons sugar
- 2-3 dried red chili peppers
- 1 5 cm / 2 in square piece of konbu seaweed, or 1 teaspoon konbu dashi stock granules (or regular dashi stock granules if you don't mind it being non-vegetarian)

Directions

- Place all the vegetables in a medium sized bowl and add salt before you whisk until they start to wilt.
- Now add all the ingredients into a container that is non-reactive and after giving it a really good shake,

put this container into the refrigerator for a whole night before you place it in any bento boxes.

WALNUT MISO TOPPING FOR VEGETABLES

Ingredients

- 1/2 cup (about 1 oz / 33 g) shelled walnut kernels
- 1 Tbsp. miso of your choice
- 1 Tbsp. mirin
- 1/2 Tbsp. raw cane sugar - regular white sugar is fine

Directions

- Cook walnuts in hot oil over medium heat until brown and then rub them to remove the outer skin.
- Now crush it with the help of a food processor very finely and combine it with mirin, miso and sugar.
- Mix it very thoroughly before you place them in an airtight container for about a full week.
- You can use it with any other bento.

BROWN RICE PORRIDGE WITH AZUKI BEANS

Ingredients

- 1 cup (240ml) brown rice, rinsed
- 3 tablespoons dry azuki beans
- a pinch of salt
- 5 cups (5x the amount of rice) water - try 7 cups for a looser porridge

Directions

- Place everything mentioned in the ingredients above into pot and let it stand for the whole night.
- Now bring this to boil at high heat before you turn down the heat to medium and cook for about one full hour while keeping the lid on.
- You can also make this in advance for bento and freeze it. (When you want to use it, you can take it out and heat it in a

microwave after putting some water into it).

MEATBALL BENTO

Ingredients

- Steamed rice
- Meatballs (Purchase in freezer section)
- Ham
- Hard boiled eggs (made previous night)
- Steamed broccoli (parboiled previous night)
- Cherry tomatoes
- Strawberries
- Mandarin orange

Directions

- Put steamed rice in the bento box so that it fills half of it and let it cool down.
- Now take out meatballs and heat them in a frying pan before transferring them to a plate and cooling it down.
- In this time, you need to make Ham and set it aside for later use, or place pieces of deli ham.

- Now pack all this food in the bento box, plus remaining ingredients.
- You need to make sure that everything is cool enough before you close the box.

SANSHOKU BENTO

Ingredients

- Soboro Don
- Salted Salmon
- Shredded nori sheet
- Strawberries

Directions

- After filling 2/3 of the bento box with rice, add salmon flakes, ground chicken and scramble egg on top of this.
- Also sprinkle some shredded nori over it.
- Now place strawberries in 1/3 of the box.
- You need to make sure that everything is cool enough before you close the box.

Hamburger Steak Bento

Ingredients

- White Rice
- Beef Steak
- Pre-blanched broccoli
- Tomato
- Celery
- Cooked corn
- Furikake

Directions

- Put rice in ½ of the bento box and let it cool down completely.
- Now heat up beef steak in a frying pan until you see that it is heated through.
- Now put this in your bento box in a silicon cup.
- Now put corn, tomato, broccoli and celery in the box.
- Also sprinkle some furikake on rice.
- You need to make sure that everything is cool enough before you close the box.

Mushroom, Carrot, Sriracha Veggie Dumplings

Ingredients

- 3 tablespoon olive oil
- 1 pound(s) mushrooms, finely chopped
- 4 cloves garlic, minced
- half cup shredded carrot
- 1 1/4 cup shredded cabbage
- 1 tablespoon soy sauce
- 2 teaspoon sesame oil
- 1 teaspoon sriracha
- 1/8 teaspoon black pepper
- 1 green onion, light and dark green part thinly sliced

Directions

- Cook garlic and mushrooms in hot olive oil for 10 minutes and stir in carrot and cabbage before cooking it for 2 more minutes and stirring in soy sauce, green onion,

sriracha, sesame oil and black
pepper.
- Fold up the wrappers around this
  mixture and cook all these
  dumplings in hot oil for 4
  minutes before stirring in water
  and cooking for another three
  minutes.
- Serve with soy sauce.

PORK DUMPLING REMIX

Ingredients

- 1 portion of Basic Yeast Dough
- 2 tablespoon oyster sauce
- 2 tablespoon hoisin sauce
- 2 tablespoon soy sauce
- 2 tablespoon sesame oil
- 3 tablespoon Chinese rice wine / sherry
- 6 tablespoon sugar
- 2 tablespoon cornstarch
- 6 tablespoon water
- 1 pound(s)barbeque pork (char siu), diced small 1/4 inch cubes
- half cup dried onion flakes soaked in 1/4 cup of water
- 2 tablespoon sesame seeds, roasted
- 20 pieces of 2 x 2 wax paper.

Directions

- Form a basic yeast based dough for the steamed buns and cover it up.
- Heat up a mixture of all the wet ingredients and stir in diced pork, sesame seeds and dried onion before cooking it for a few minutes.
- Fill up portions of dough with this mixture and fold it up, while sealing the edges tightly.
- Let buns stand as it is for 20 minutes and steam it for 15 minutes (with a colander).
- Serve.

Tofu Shrimp

Ingredients

- 8 ounce(s) shelled and deveined shrimp
- 1 tablespoon finely chopped yellow chives
- 7-8 pieces tofu skin, cut into 6×6-inch pieces
- Oil, for deep-frying
- Worcestershire sauce or mayonnaise
- 1/2 teaspoon chicken bouillon powder
- 1/4 teaspoon salt
- 1/2 teaspoon Shaoxing wine
- 1/2 teaspoon sesame oil
- 3 dashes white pepper powder
- 1/2 teaspoon oil
- 1 heaping teaspoon potato starch or cornstarch*
- 1/2 tablespoon egg white

Directions

- Coat sliced up shrimp with a mixture of all the ingredients of seasoning and fold tofu skin around this mixture
- Now cook these shrimp rolls in hot oil until golden brown from all sides.
- Serve with mayonnaise.

Asian Pancakes

Ingredients

Dough:

- 1 cup all-purpose flour
- 1 cup bread flour
- 2 teaspoon sugar
- 1/4 teaspoon salt
- 1/2 cup hot/warm water (150° F)
- 1/4 cup cold/room-temperature water
- 1/4 cup vegetable oil
- Scallion oil and fillings
- 2 cups diced scallions, divided
- 1/2 cup vegetable oil
- 1 teaspoon salt
- 1 teaspoon ground white pepper, divided into 1/2 teaspoon each
- 1/4 teaspoon ground black pepper
- 1/8 teaspoon baking soda
- Coarse sea salt, to taste

- More vegetable oil for frying

Directions

- Combine all-purpose flour, salt, bread flour and sugar in a mixer, and mix for 1 minute while stirring in a half cup of hot water. Then add in some cold water before stirring vegetable oil and mixing for 5 minutes.
- Let it stand as it is for 1 hour.
- Blend a mixture of diced scallions, vegetable oil, salt, half teaspoon of ground white pepper and quarter teaspoon ground black pepper until smooth, and combine baking soda and three tablespoons of this mixture separately in a bowl before placing both these mixtures in the fridge and mixing scallion and ground white pepper in another bowl.
- Divide dough into 4 portions and fill it up with all three fillings before folding it up tightly.

- Now cook in hot oil until golden brown from all sides and brush it with scallion oil.
- Serve.

Five Spice Dumpling

Ingredients

FILLING:

- 1 tablespoon minced garlic
- 1 1/2 teaspoon minced fresh ginger
- 3 tablespoon bruised and minced lemongrass
- 1 tablespoon gluten-free soy sauce
- 1 tablespoon untoasted sesame oil
- 1 teaspoon Kosher Salt
- 1/4 teaspoon Chinese five spice powder
- 4 ounces or 1 cup, packed whole Napa cabbage leaves, chopped
- 1/4 cup sliced scallions
- 1/2 pound ground chicken thighs

WRAP:

- 120 grams (1 cup) millet flour, plus more for rolling
- 120 grams (1 cup) Garbanzo-Fava Flour
- 96 grams (1/2 cup) Potato Starch
- 64 grams (1/2 cup) Arrowroot Starch
- 18 grams (2 tablespoon) Xanthan Gum
- 312 grams (11 ounces or 1 1/4 cups plus 2 tablespoon) Boiling Water

Cooking Related:

- Peanut or Grapeseed Oil
- Chili Oil (spicy)
- Plum sauce (sweet, sour)
- Soy-scallion dipping sauce

Directions

- Combine minced garlic, five spice powder, cabbage, scallions and chicken very thoroughly before refrigerating it for an hour.

- Form dough from a mixture of millet flour and xanthan gum that is mixed using an electric mixer on medium speed for 2 minutes before kneading it into one lump.
- Roll it up and cut it with a cookie cutter before filling it up with the prepared mixture and folding it tightly.
- Steam these dumpling for 10 minutes and then fry for 2 more mins to give it a good golden brown color
- Serve with any type of dipping sauce that you like.

BBQ Pork

(Char Siu)

Ingredients

- 1 pound whole pork belly, skin removed
- 2 tablespoon Chinese rice wine or dry sherry
- 2 tablespoon dark soy sauce, or substitute regular soy sauce
- 2 tablespoon sugar
- 2 cloves garlic, minced
- half tablespoon hoisin sauce
- half teaspoon five-spice powder
- 2 tablespoon honey

Directions

- Set your oven at 325 degrees before doing anything else.
- Coat pork belly with a mixture of rice wine, dark soy sauce, sugar, five-spice powder, hoisin sauce

and garlic very thoroughly before refrigerating for 3 hours.
- Place it in a big pan after brushing with some honey. Roast for 45 minutes.
- Cool it down and cut into small pieces.
- Serve.

STEAM BUNS WITH SWEET POTATO

Ingredients

- 1/2 tablespoon yeast
- 1/3 cup warm water
- 1/2 teaspoon sugar

2nd:

- 1/3 cup sweet potato
- 1 cup cake flour
- 4 tablespoon sugar
- 4 tablespoon oil
- Pinch of salt

Directions

- Let a mixture of sugar, yeast and warm water stand as it is for 20 minutes
- Steam sweet potato and mash it before mixing it with the yeast mixture and all the ingredients

mentioned under 2nd with an electric mixer for 10 minutes.

- Refrigerate for 1 hour and divide this dough into 3 equal portions before cutting it into small cylindrical shapes.
- Steam for 15 minutes.

SHRIMP DUMPLINGS

Ingredients

- 6 ounce(s) fresh deveined shrimp
- 1 pound(s) ground pork
- 1 cup dried shiitake mushrooms
- 3 green onions, thinly sliced, white portions removed
- 2 egg whites
- 1 1/2 teaspoon low sodium soy sauce
- 1 1/2 tablespoon cooking sherry
- 1/2 teaspoon sesame oil
- 2 teaspoon cornstarch
- 1 teaspoon sugar
- 1 teaspoon chicken bouillon
- 1/4 teaspoon white pepper
- wonton or siu mai wrappers
- non-stick spray
- mini cubed carrots, thinly sliced green onions, chili sauce, or salmon caviar eggs to garnish (optional)

Directions

- Soak shiitake mushrooms in warm for 30 minutes and drain it before cutting it into small pieces and blending it until smooth.
- Now stir in ground pork, chopped shrimp, green onions, sugar, egg whites, soy, sesame oil, cornstarch, sherry, bouillon and pepper, and combine everything thoroughly before filling up wrappers with this mixture and folding it up real tight.
- Steam these dumplings for 12 minutes.
- Garnish with carrots, chili sauce and green onion

EGG TREAT

Ingredients

- 1 pack frozen pie crust
- 2/3 cup granulated sugar
- 1 half cups water
- 9 eggs
- half teaspoon vanilla extract
- 1 cup evaporated milk
- mini tart pan

Directions

- Set your oven at 400 degrees before doing anything else.
- Combine beaten eggs, a mixture of water and sugar, vanilla extract and milk very thoroughly.
- Put premade pie crust into tart pan and pour in egg mixture but not filling it fully.
- Bake this in the preheated oven for about 20 minutes.
- Serve.

Easy Five Spice Squid

Ingredients

- 1 pound squid tentacles
- half cup cornflour
- half cup plain flour
- 1 teaspoon ground black pepper
- 1 teaspoon ground white pepper
- 1 teaspoon Chinese five spice
- sea salt
- 3 cloves garlic, minced
- 3 red chilli, sliced
- 3 stalks spring onion, sliced
- Vegetable oil for frying

Directions

- Coat squid tentacles with a mixture of white pepper, corn flour, regular flour, black pepper and salt.
- Cook garlic, spring onion and chili in hot oil for 30 seconds and

stir in tentacles before cooking all
this for 2 minutes.

- Sprinkle garlic and chili mixture
  on top, and serve with steamed
  jasmine rice.
- Serve.

Rice Rolls

Ingredients

Rice Noodle Mix:

- 2 1/2 cups rice flour
- 5 cups water
- 1 tablespoon sesame oil
- 2 tablespoon cooking oil
- 1/4 teaspoon fine salt

Filling:

- half a pound BBQ pork (Char Siu), diced
- Spring onions, sliced
- Soy sauce and sesame oil to drizzle over to serve

Directions

- Combine all the ingredients of rice noodle mix very thoroughly before microwaving a spoonful of this mixture for two minutes.
- Now fill up dough straight out of microwave with BBQ pork and spring onions before folding it up.
- Serve with soy sauce, spring onions and sesame on top.

Pork Puffs

Ingredients

Filling:

- 3 ounce(s) ground pork
- 1 teaspoon soy sauce
- 1 teaspoon minced fresh ginger
- 3 ounce(s) shrimp, peeled and deveined
- Salt
- Pepper
- Pinch sugar
- 1 teaspoon cornstarch
- 1/2 teaspoon sesame oil
- 1-1/2 teaspoon oyster sauce
- 1 teaspoon sherry
- 1 tablespoon water
- 1 tablespoon canola or peanut oil
- 2 or 3 scallions, white and green parts, chopped

DOUGH:

- 1 large taro root (3/4 to 1 pound(s))
- 1/3 cup wheat starch
- 1/3 cup boiling water (approximately)
- Pinch salt
- 1-1/4 teaspoon sugar
- 1/4 cup lard or solid vegetable shortening, at room temperature

Directions

- Combine salt, sugar, some pepper, sesame oil, oyster sauce, cornstarch, sherry and water very thoroughly, and coat shrimp with salt.
- Cook pork coated with soy sauce and ginger in hot oil for a few minutes and stir in shrimp before pouring in sauce mixture and stirring in scallion.
- Turn the heat off and refrigerate for several hours.

- Peel taro root and chop it up into small pieces.
- Steam taro for 45 minutes and mash it before mixing it with a mixture of wheat starch and water, salt and sugar.
- Refrigerate for 2 hours.
- Cut into twelve dough pieces and fill it up with the prepared mixture before folding it up.
- Fry dumpling in hot oil for 3 three or until brown.
- Serve.

Easy Wrappers for Dumplings

Ingredient

- 1 pound All-Purpose Flour
- half teaspoon Sea Salt
- 1 1/3 cups of Water

Directions

- Form dough from a mixture of salt, flour and water, and divide into 4 pieces before covering it up and refrigerating it until used.

Vegetable Rolls

Ingredients

- 2 tablespoon vegetable oil
- 1 medium brown onion, diced (1 cup)
- 1 tablespoon garlic, finely chopped
- 2 teaspoon ginger, grated
- 1 ounce(s) dried shiitake mushrooms, rinsed, dried, stems cut, diced
- 1 tablespoon cooking wine
- 2 carrots, shredded
- 1 red bell pepper, diced
- 1/2 small head of cabbage, diced
- 1 teaspoon sesame oil
- 1/2 teaspoon white pepper
- 1 teaspoon sugar
- 3 tablespoon vegetarian oyster sauce
- 2 green onions, sliced finely
- 12 large sheets of phyllo dough, thawed and kept moist

- vegetable oil spray
- Sweet & Sour Sauce

Directions

- Set your oven at 425 degrees before doing anything else.
- Cook onion, ginger and garlic in hot oil for 1 minute and stir in mushroom before cooking it for 2 minutes and stirring in sherry.
- Cook it for a few more minutes and stir in shredded carrots and some sliced red bell pepper before cooking all this for three minutes and stirring sliced cabbage.
- Cook for three minutes and then stir in sesame oil, sugar, white pepper and vegetarian oyster sauce before cooking on high heat for four minutes
- Cool it down and stir in green onion before folding this mixture around phyllo and sealing it up tightly.

- Make 12 vegie rolls.
- Bake this in the preheated oven for about 10 minutes or until golden brown from all sides.
- Serve with Sweet & Sour Sauce.

ASPARAGUS DUMPLINGS

Ingredients

Filling:

- 6 ounce(s) peeled, deveined shrimp, chopped
- 1 teaspoon soy sauce
- 1 1/2 teaspoon sherry
- 1/2 teaspoon sesame oil
- 2 tablespoon vegetable oil spread
- 1 teaspoon white sugar
- 1 teaspoon salt
- 1/8 teaspoon white pepper
- 1 1/2 teaspoon cornstarch
- 3 large cloves garlic, crushed
- 15 green asparagus stalks, white tough base removed, chopped into 1/4" pieces

Wrapping:

- 20 dumpling wrappers, square-shaped

Finishes:

- 5 extra stalks of asparagus, for making asparagus ribbons
- soy sauce
- chili oil

Directions

- Mix all the filling ingredients thoroughly and fill up the dumpling wrapper to form 20 dumplings.
- Peel out some very thin ribbons from asparagus and wrap these ribbons around the dumpling before placing dumpling in the bamboo steamer.
- Steam for 10 minutes and serve it immediately.

INDO-CHINESE PUFFS

Ingredients

- 1 pound(s) ground chicken
- 3 tablespoon vegetable oil
- 1/2 brown onion, finely chopped
- 2 tablespoon red curry paste
- 2 tablespoon Asian curry powder
- 1/2 teaspoon salt
- 1 tablespoon soy sauce
- 1/2 teaspoon sesame oil
- 2 tablespoon sugar
- 1/4 teaspoon black pepper
- 1 tablespoon rice wine or sherry
- 1/4 cup chopped cilantro
- 3 green onions, green parts only, thinly sliced
- 1 package puff pastry, thawed
- 1 egg mixed with 1 teaspoon of water
- tablespoon sesame seeds

Directions

- Cook chopped onion in hot oil for a few minutes and stir in curry paste, salt and curry powder, and cook for another 2 minutes before stirring in ground chicken and cooking over high heat.
- Stir in soy, black pepper, sesame oil and sugar, and add rice wine when the chicken tender.
- When the filling is cool enough, stir in chopped green onion and sliced cilantro.
- Set your oven at 425 degrees and fill up the puff pastry with this mixture before folding it up tightly and brushing it with egg wash.
- Sprinkle some sesame seeds.
- Bake in the preheated oven for about 17 minutes or until golden brown.
- Serve.

Mushroom Dumplings

Ingredients

- Napa cabbage leaves, sliced thinly
- 1 medium carrot, peeled and shredded
- 1 teaspoon salt
- 1 ounce(s) shiitake mushrooms, stems removed and diced into 1/4" pieces
- 1 tablespoon vegetable oil
- 2 teaspoon light soy sauce
- 8 ounce(s)of firm tofu, well-drained and squeezed into a course purée
- 2 tablespoon vegetarian stir-fry sauce (also called vegetarian oyster sauce, I used Lee Kum Kee brand)
- 1 teaspoon sesame oil
- 1/4 teaspoon white pepper
- 1/2 teaspoon sugar
- 1/4 teaspoon grated garlic

- extra Napa cabbage leaves and shiitake mushrooms, for serving on the side (optional)
- 30 round potsticker wrappers
- small cup of water for sealing potstickers
- cups of water
- green tea bags

Directions:

- Cook mushroom in hot oil for a minute and stir in soy sauce before cooking it for 5 minutes.
- Coat Napa cabbage and carrot with salt and let it stand as it for 10 minutes before draining off excess water.
- Combine Napa, carrots, tofu, vegetarian oyster sauce, sesame oil, white pepper, sugar, garlic and mushrooms very thoroughly before filling up the dumpling wrapper and folding it up.
- Steam for 10 mins.

MAGGIE'S FAVORITE DUMPLINGS

Ingredients

Dumplings

- 2 teaspoon canola oil
- 4 cloves garlic, minced (about 4 teaspoon)
- 2 teaspoon minced fresh ginger
- 1 pound(s) eggplant, peeled and finely chopped (4 cups)
- 2 tablespoon low-sodium soy sauce
- 1 tablespoon black bean sauce
- 1 teaspoon dark sesame oil
- 4 tablespoon minced cilantro
- Cornstarch for dusting pan
- 24 wrappers

Chili Sauce

- 2 tablespoon low-sodium soy sauce
- 1 tablespoon fresh lemon juice
- 1 teaspoon brown sugar or honey
- 1 teaspoon dark sesame oil
- 1 clove garlic, minced (about 1 teaspoon)
- 1 teaspoon grated fresh ginger
- 1 red jalapeño

Directions

- Cook garlic and ginger in hot oil for one minute, and add eggplant before cooking it over high heat for 5 minutes and stirring in soy sauce, cilantro, bean sauce and sesame oil.
- Fold up this mixture around wrappers and refrigerate for 24 hours.
- Steam for 8 minutes in metal steamer inserts.
- Serve with chili sauce.

Thanks for Reading! Now Let's Try some Sushi and Dump Dinners....

Send the Book!

To grab this **box set** simply follow the link mentioned above, or tap the book cover.

This will take you to a page where you can simply enter your email address and a PDF version of the **box set** will be emailed to you.

I hope you are ready for some serious cooking!

<u>Send the Book!</u>

You will also receive updates about all my new books when they are free.

Also don't forget to like and subscribe on the social networks. I love meeting my readers. Links to all my profiles are below so please click and connect :)

<u>Facebook</u>

<u>Twitter</u>

Come On...
Let's Be Friends :)

I adore my readers and love connecting with them socially. Please follow the links below so we can connect on Facebook, Twitter, and Google+.

Facebook

Twitter

I also have a blog that I regularly update for my readers so check it out below.

My Blog

CAN I ASK A FAVOUR?

If you found this book interesting, or have otherwise found any benefit in it. Then may I ask that you post a review of it on Amazon? Nothing excites me more than new reviews, especially reviews which suggest new topics for writing. I do read all reviews and I always factor feedback into my newer works.

So if you are willing to take ten minutes to write what you sincerely thought about this book then please visit our Amazon page and post your opinions.

Again thank you!

INTERESTED IN OTHER EASY COOKBOOKS?

Everything is easy! Check out my Amazon Author page for more great cookbooks:

For a complete listing of all my books please see my author page.

Made in the USA
Lexington, KY
27 August 2018